Branches of the Banyan

Branches of the Banyan

OBSERVATIONS ON
THE CHURCH IN SOUTHERN ASIA

Edited by

ADDISON J. EASTMAN

Friendship Press • New York

Library of Congress Catalog Card No. 63-8683

TEXT TYPE: ELECTRA 11/13
COMPOSITION: SOWERS PRINTING COMPANY
LEBANON, PENNSYLVANIA
FORMAT: LOUISE E. JEFFERSON

Contents

Branches of the Banyan

AN INTRODUCTORY VIEW

Everywhere in Southern Asia the banyan tree is a familiar sight. Its huge branches spread a haven of shade for the weary traveler, a meeting place for friends, or a site for an outdoor school or a village shrine. Often an earthen water jar sits nearby on a stone slab for the friend or stranger who may wish to drink. In some villages the banyan—its name means "tree of the merchants"—provides shelter for the weekly bazaar or the farmers' market.

The trees are known for their beauty and their growth to mighty proportions. One of them in India is famous as the Calcutta Banyan; its branches spread so far that several thousand people have been able to meet beneath it at one time.

The banyan tree can be a symbol of the church in Southern Asia. Recently a Christian botany professor from Ceylon, commenting on this symbolism, said: "Don't forget those wonderful aerial roots that hang down from the branches until they reach the ground to take hold of the soil and grow new trees. They are like the young church in my country. Missionaries from the West planted the seed and it has grown, but today the church in Ceylon is trying to send down its own roots into the soil of the country. Only now are those roots beginning to reach the ground, where tender shoots are seeking for a place to take hold. We know that, like the banyan, they will succeed."

This book tells something of the story of the Christian church as it sends its roots down into the soil of Southern Asia. This section of the world is a vast area, stretching from the Indian Ocean in the south to the Himalaya Mountains in the north. It includes four nations—India, Pakistan, Ceylon, and Nepal—which, while they stand within the same latitude lines on our map, differ in many major respects. Each has its own distinctive history and cultural patterns as well as its unique contribution to make in today's world.

North Americans probably know India best because of its size, its famous leaders like Mahatma Gandhi and Jawaharlal Nehru, and its role in world affairs. The meeting of the World Council of Churches in New Delhi in 1961 did much to bring the country particular attention from Protestant and Orthodox Christians. India is slightly more than one-third the size of the United States but has almost three times as many people. Although Indian culture and tradition can be traced back to times before Christ, the Republic of India may rightfully be considered a new member of the family of nations because it gained independence from Great Britain only in 1947. Today India is in population the largest democracy in the world, a sovereign democratic republic within the British Commonwealth but without allegiance to the British crown.

Next in terms of size is Pakistan, a nation divided into two sections, East and West, with a thousand miles of Indian territory between them. Pakistan came into being at the same time as the Republic of India. It consists of areas that had been primarily Muslim during the period of British rule. The 70 million Muslims feared being a minority in a Hindu-dominated nation. The partition of the subcontinent was accompanied by violent conflict between Muslims and Hindus; thousands of men, women, and children were slaughtered. The two nations still are on uneasy terms with one another. Today Pakistan, which means "Land of the Pure," is the home of about 94 million people. It is the fifth most populous country and the largest Muslim nation in the world. It too is a member of the British Commonwealth.

At the southern tip of India lies the beautiful island of Ceylon, which is about the size of West Virginia. Its population of 19 million is made up mainly of Sinhalese and Tamil-speaking people. Its independence was granted by Great Britain in 1948; it is within the Commonwealth.

The mountain Kingdom of Nepal lies along the northern edge of Southern Asia. It is famous not for its geographic breadth but for the towering height of peaks like Mount Everest and Kanchenjunga. Nepal, too, may be called a new nation, for though it has long been an independent monarchy, a revolution in 1950-51 overthrew the century-old Rana regime and laid foundations for democracy. A new constitution was drawn up and under King Mahendra, the first parliamentary government was elected in 1959. The population of Nepal is about nine million persons.

These nations are seeking economic and social development

under severe difficulties. One problem is the sheer number of people and what is commonly known as the "population explosion." Today the population of these four countries exceeds 500 million, which is more than that of all the twenty-two nations of the Western hemisphere combined. According to United Nations sources the population of India increased from 345 million in 1947 to nearly 445 million in 1961. It is expected to reach 625 million by 1976. Ceylon's population is increasing at the rate of 3 per cent per year, and it is estimated that in twenty-five years the nation will have twice as many people as it does today. But the population boom can best be recognized not by reading figures but by walking down crowded streets like those of Calcutta in the late evening and seeing hundreds of people sleeping on the sidewalks and in doorways. It staggers even the steadiest mind to try to comprehend the implications of these millions of people in terms of their needs for food, clothing, shelter, and jobs.

Western observers sometimes suppose that family planning will be the quick answer, but many Asian leaders feel that no swift solution is in sight. Governments and volunteer agencies are already engaged in large-scale family planning programs, but much more is involved than the mere introduction of birth control techniques. For the people of Asia, family planning is a new way of life that will become a part of their culture only slowly.

Another problem is the need to develop economic strength swiftly. All the nations of Southern Asia have undertaken long-term plans and made remarkable progress in recent years with the aid of other countries, including the United States and Canada. But food production and national income have to increase still more rapidly to keep pace with the ever-growing population. In spite of the tremendous gains already made through new agricultural techniques and the introduction of basic industries, the standard of living is still tragically low. These nations are essentially agricultural, with about three-fourths of their populations living on the land. Yet the output of the farmer in Southern Asia is said to be near the lowest in the world. The average annual income is somewhere near seventy dollars. East Pakistan is probably the most depressed area, only one-fifth the size of West Pakistan but with twenty million more people. It is commonly referred to as the "poorest land in Asia." Recently a Christian who lives there reported ironically that his country has suffered "repeated natural disasters which have upset a normally unstable economy."

In education as in economic development, the people of Southern Asia are engaged in a desperate race. Their governments are working constantly to provide education for all the people, but illiteracy is still very high. Much money, time, and effort are being invested in literacy campaigns and new schools at primary, secondary, and college level. One of the top priorities in plans for educational development has been given to the training of teachers. While most teachers are trained within their own countries, many have been sent to schools in Europe and North America.

The fourth major problem is that of disunity. Although Southern Asia's nations are close neighbors, tension frequently exists among them in matters of trade, immigration, and boundaries. For example, India and Pakistan have not yet found agreement in their dispute over Kashmir and live in constant fear of each other's growing military strength. But even within each country there have been extreme difficulties in welding national unity out of diversities in religions, classes, regions, and language groups. Problems of communalism—of a group's staying separate from others in the same nation—sometimes seem as difficult to

surmount as Everest itself. The plea for a separate state is often
made by minority groups like the Sikhs in India. In Nepal, small
political factions have been rebelling against the government because they feel their interests are not adequately represented.
Linguistic loyalties cause grave concern. India is a nation divided
by several hundred languages, fourteen of which are recognized
in the constitution as regional languages. Many people have been
killed there and in Ceylon during riots over the language issue.

The Christian church, in seeking to witness in this vast and
complex area of the world, meets three other major religions.
Hinduism is the faith of more than 85 per cent of Indian people.
Pakistan has the largest Islamic population in the world. Ceylon
is regarded by many as the intellectual center of Theravāda
Buddhism, and in the period since World War II has actively
sought to revive the faith and spread it throughout the world.
In Nepal, Hinduism and Buddhism are at many points insep-
arable in the life of the average person. The king of Nepal is
considered an incarnation of the Hindu deity, Vishnu.

Visitors to Southern Asia find the Christian church at many
different stages of growth, meeting its challenges in its own way.
In South India, for instance, the Syrian Church prides itself on
its long centuries of history and the tradition that it was founded
by the Apostle Thomas around the year 58. In contrast, Nepal
was virtually closed to the Christian witness until as late as 1951,
so that its oldest congregation has been meeting for only a few
short years.

The church in these lands faces many difficulties. Christians
are but a tiny minority. In India there are about 15 million,
less than 4 per cent of the total population. In Pakistan they
number about 733,000, or less than one per cent, and in Nepal
it is estimated that there are less than two hundred Christians.
Ceylon is something of an exception. About 9 per cent of the

population may be considered Christian, of which more than three-fourths are Roman Catholic. Although the governments of Southern Asia try to insure freedom to minority groups, they do not always succeed in doing so, especially on the local level. Thus Christians sometimes feel that they have more than average difficulty in finding jobs, housing, and educational opportunities. In some instances laws regarding the right to change one's religion have brought imprisonment to Christians and made their evangelistic task difficult indeed.

In most places, however, Christians are free not only to worship as they choose but to proclaim the gospel openly to their non-Christian countrymen. India's Prime Minister Nehru once told a Christian gathering: "It stands to reason that any faith whose roots are strong and healthy should spread; and to interfere with that right to spread seems to me to be a blow at the roots themselves."

The purpose of this book is to examine certain aspects of the church's life in a way that will help us to cross cultural barriers and to experience a new sense of identification with Christians of India, Pakistan, Ceylon, and Nepal. To do this, a wide variety of material has been brought together. It comes to us from people who have first hand experience in the areas they write about.

To gain new insights into the life of the church in Southern Asia we could begin at many different points, but these observations begin with a look at the church as it seeks to minister to a few of the varied needs in Southern Asia. Next comes a group of sketches of Christian leaders, followed by a section focused on one particular area of Christian concern—family life. The fourth group of selections deals with some unique qualities of church life. The final chapter ties the threads together and suggests some possible lines of future direction.

As we move from one selection to another, we may find ourselves at one moment standing in the waiting room of a Christion medical center, with Hindu patients crowded all around us. Next we may feel involved with members of a young Christian family who have recently moved from a village to a city and do not yet understand the forces changing their lives. Again we shall be seeking to comprehend the spiritual disciplines of a Christian ashram. Or we shall sit with serious young students as they try to discover ways of expressing the gospel so that their Muslim neighbors will understand it.

In the process of sharing, even for a brief moment, the life of our Christian brethren in Southern Asia we are bound to see ourselves in a new light. We shall probably find that we are forced to ask fundamental questions about our own faith and about our beliefs regarding the church and its place in the particular form of Western culture that has been our heritage. New insights and perspectives on our own situations can come in the process of sharing Christian love and concern across national, racial, and cultural boundaries. Thus we engage with other members of the household of God in a process in which we both give and receive.

"A visible symbol of Christian presence"

Making Jesus Christ known among the millions of village people is a great responsibility of the church in Southern Asia. Sister Eileen Bending of the Church of South India describes one way of attempting to accomplish the task. Because the method is an old one, which some people might believe should be abandoned, there is value in recalling a comment by D. T. Niles of Ceylon. While it is wrong to think that being a missionary means only preaching the gospel under a palm tree, he said, it is equally wrong to think that being a missionary may not mean preaching the gospel under a palm tree.

The Gospel in Rayalaseema

It is four o'clock in the afternoon. The village in the Rayalaseema area of South India is quiet, most of the able-bodied men and women being at work in the fields. A few old people sit and gossip under a tree or lie asleep on their rope beds in the shade of their houses. The mothers of small babies are already pounding grain in preparation for the evening meal. From the tiny, one-room school-cum-church building in the center of the Christians' houses comes a babble of voices as two teachers attempt to teach five classes of children ranging from five to eleven years of age. The voices of the children studying aloud their alphabet, their multiplication tables, some morality verses, and other contents of their few tattered textbooks are echoed by the voices of other children outside the school building. They have never been submitted to this discipline but instead have been given the responsibility of looking after younger brothers and sisters, or of gathering twigs or cattle manure for fuel, or of minding the goats, buffaloes, and cows that wander in search of pasture in the surrounding fields.

A bullock cart comes in sight, raising a cloud of dust. It is seen by the children, and as it comes closer they run shouting to greet the woman missionary, the Indian Biblewoman and her untrained companion, and the young widow on probation for Biblewomen's training. The visitors clamber out of the cart and stretch their aching limbs after journeying all day, first in a very ancient bus and then the last few miles by bullock cart. The shouts of the children bring the teachers out of the school and they greet the travelers. Eager hands reach into the cart, seize the strange assortment of bedding, camp cots, book box, food sack, flannelgraph board, lamps, and medicine case and carry them into the school building. The new arrivals are taken to the teacher's house and his wife (who is assistant teacher) leaves her post to fetch them brass vessels full of refreshing water to wash their faces, hands, and feet. She then prepares sweet, hot coffee to revive them after the journey.

After exchange of news the women go into the school building at five o'clock when school is over and teach the children an action song and then a Bible story illustrated with flannelgraph pictures. The Hindu children who have attended the school all day stay and take part in this and also in the games that follow in the street afterward. Gradually the mothers and fathers of the children return from the fields, carrying on their heads large bundles of grass for their buffaloes or of wood for fuel. They pause awhile to watch their children at play and to shout encouragement or advice to them. Then the herds of buffaloes, cows, and goats come back from their meager pasture, raising clouds of dust and making further play impossible. Tired bullocks, who have worked all day in the fields, return to the houses they share with their owners, the bells round their necks tinkling cheerfully.

The Biblewomen now visit all the Christian houses. These were formerly the outcaste quarters and lie outside the main village. Many of the houses are built only of mud and thatch. They are easily erected and even more easily destroyed if fire sweeps the village. A few families have better houses built of local stone, with flat roofs and no windows. The Biblewomen greet each family in turn, asking after those who were sick when they last came to the village four or five months previously, making suitable comments about babies who have been born since then, and calling all the women to come to a meeting after the evening meal is over.

As darkness falls tiny oil lamps are lit in the houses and the church bell (a length of railway track) is rung. The teacher conducts evening prayers for the small group of adults and the large group of children who come. Most of the women are busy pounding grain and preparing evening food for their families. Some of the men are feeding their cattle or drawing water from the well. Others sit on the raised stone platform under a tree in the center of the village and smoke cheap tobacco twists and talk over the events of the day.

After eating the rice and curry meal they have brought with them, the Biblewomen ring the church bell again and gradually the women gather. Many of them bring babies on their hips and put the children to sleep on the floor in front of them. After working all day in the fields, the rather stuffy atmosphere and the dim lighting in the church make the women feel very sleepy. A few unashamedly give up the struggle and lean against the wall and sleep. But most manage to keep themselves awake by joining in the singing of familiar, well-loved songs and the learning of new songs. The singing is followed by prayer and then a lesson about the Christian faith, Christian family life, or the objectives of the Women's Fellowship of the Church of South India, into which the women are to be received after more preparation. The talk is illustrated with flat pictures or flannelgraph, rather inadequately illuminated by hurricane lanterns. Halfway through the talk a group of Hindu women arrive. Place is made for them and they sit apart from the others. The Biblewoman adjusts her talk to meet their needs.

The women stream out of the church after the meeting. The air is cool and fresh outside and there is a lovely clear moonlit sky. Someone asks for dancing and the request is taken up by many others. The women form themselves into a circle and, to the accompaniment of a Christian song sung by one of the Biblewomen and repeated by everyone, they do a traditional village dance with hand-clapping and rhythmic stamping of the feet. The Hindu women sit and watch and listen.

The Biblewomen have come to stay in the village for a week and during that time they will visit the Christian homes every day and try to give personal help and teaching to each family. They will sell Bibles, New Testaments, Gospels, hymn books, and other Christian literature to the Christians, to the Hindu children who attend the school, and to the Hindus whose homes they visit and to whom they preach the gospel. People will come and ask for medical help and they will give what aid they can, using the opportunity to tell about Jesus, the Great Physician. Every day they will teach the children and the women, and probably on Sunday the teacher will ask them to conduct worship for the whole congregation. They will remind the Christian women of a three-day summer school to be run for them and other women in the area during the hot weather when there is no field work. They forewarn them that they will be coming to collect offerings of grain for this. The women are enthusiastic and promise to give the grain. Some say that they will walk the seven miles to the village where the summer school has been arranged, so that they may enjoy the fellowship, teaching, worship, and fun together with women from other villages. So the week passes and it is time for the Biblewomen to move on to another village. The Christian women say good-bye with regret. In the two or three years since the Biblewomen began their visits, real friendship has been established.

Adapted from a monthly missionary letter by Sister Eileen Bending.

For many years the Himalayan Kingdom of Nepal was closed to the rest of the world. Outsiders called it "The Last Home of Mystery." In 1951, however, a change of government opened the country's doors. Since then Nepal has sought outside help in a sweeping effort to gain the benefits of modern technology for its nine million citizens.

Among the many agencies providing this assistance today is the United Mission to Nepal, the first Christian mission to enter the country in many years. The group is notable also because its members come from and are supported by Christians of many different denominations and countries.

At first, the mission's work was only medical but now it includes activities in education and village development. These services are combined in a program of fundamental education described by Jonathan Lindell, executive secretary of the mission.

Nepal: A Captivating Enterprise

The Nepalese government gave us permission to conduct the educational program in a rather obscure district, well back up in the mountains, about six days hike away from the big city base. Here in the Gurkha area, beside terraced fields and among scraggly woods, live 190,000 villagers in "the Middle Ages."

The first of the team to go out were three men, American, English, Nepali. Their first concern, of course, was where to locate the project. They scouted around, consulted with the governor, and then went over to a certain pass on one of the ridges that seemed suitable. The curious villagers were invited to gather the next morning to get an explanation of this "expedition" that had come among them. So under the village shade tree next morning the team members explained their program and the offer of co-operative service with the villagers. Would they invite the team to locate there? They took the matter home with them for two days and then, when the governor arrived to help with the negotiations, fifty-three village leaders from several villages of that mountain signed their names to a three-foot-long letter of invitation. It was more than an invitation; it was really a kind of covenant agreement to work with the team on the development program. To seal the matter further, the village headman sold a piece of field to the team for their first dwelling at a price fixed by the company of villagers. The program was launched.

There was not so much as a cowshed to be rented for a dwelling. The three men with their cook lived in a tent for the first six weeks, then moved for nine months into a bamboo-thatch house, and finally into a permanent stone-mud dwelling. Their first step was to hire a runner who has been going back and forth to the big city ever since, handling the lines of communication and transportation. A few days later a dozen boys sat under a tree near the tent and the school work was begun. That night people gathered after supper around the tent and listened to hymn singing and devotions, and the sharing of God's Word was started. Next morning a mother brought her burned baby, and medical work had its very humble beginnings. A villager went to the governor in the district seat and negotiated a gift of fifty trees, and the building work was under way. The men got an early introduction to the food situation when they could get locally only 10 per cent of the fruits, vegetables, and proteins that they felt they needed.

With the passing of each week and month, conditions for living and working improved. Every two to three weeks the runner arrived from his round trip and brought mail and provisions. Others brought building tools, school books, and fruit tree seedlings. As soon as living quarters in new buildings permitted, two nurses joined the team and opened a proper dispensary. Villagers helped in arranging more land purchases, in instructing the team members about local customs and rules, in forming a local education committee. A strong crew of workmen put up building after building. More team members arrived, enlarging the services and contacts of the program. The government opened a post office in the village and businessmen opened shops. Soon there was promise of an airfield to be built in the valley, three hours away. The time raced swiftly.

Now the third year is past. The team numbers fifteen. Most of the services planned in the program are well under way. Team members reckon that five years will be needed to bring the base project to that maturity and content that they would like to see. Then more attention can be given to spreading into the district. With the villagers they are constantly growing in understanding, in mutual confidence, and in affection.

The undertaking has been a thoroughly captivating enterprise from the very first hour, calling out the very fullest and best gifts and energies of all the members of the team. Their hearts have constantly been sustained by a great joy and strong confidence that God is present and working. The question has hung like a plaque on the wall of their hearts, "What can I do today to help bring new life to the people of this community?" And they have gone out among the people to work at it day and night. At the present stage of the work the members of the team are in daily personal contact with about five hundred people of the community. They deal with them in school classrooms and on the playing field, in village committee meetings, in the dispensary clinic, on beds of sickness and on house calls, in house meetings and classes, in Sunday services, in village yards and porches, on the building job, in fields and on roads, with travelers stopping by to see and visit, in earnest talks with students, with parents, officials, shopkeepers, men and women from next door and from four days away.

From the beginning the questions have come thick and fast. Will you really be childless if you plant bamboo on other than the south side of your house? . . . Yes, for sure she stole the money, even though she doesn't admit it, but what to do about it? . . . Are small eggs and potatoes better than large ones? . . . Why aren't K-notes negotiable here when they are in the big city? . . . Will it really put the people in a bad way with their gods if we enter their houses to spray against bugs? . . . Is there no other kind of fertilizer in these parts than dung? . . . When you say, "Yes, I will," what does that mean? How far can you get in real social living without Yes meaning Yes and No meaning No? . . . Can't you really read in literacy class when the moon is in eclipse? . . . It's possible to buy a few fruits and vegetables maybe six or eight times a year; shouldn't there be more of these foods in people's diets? . . . How can more of these children be released from grass cutting and cattle grazing to attend school? Suppose people do diversify their farming and raise a crop for cash sale; where can they market it for profit? . . . Can there be substantial trade and business with the outside, the flow of money and goods? Can this take place without suitable means of transportation, communication, knowledge? . . . Scabies, worms, bedbugs, rats; they're like to wear us to distraction until the bigger things fall on us: fever, the runs, broken bones, quick wearing out on the inside. Where do you begin? Do you begin with the medicine shelf, or at the home, in the school, in the legislature, with the gods, with men's minds, or where? . . . Is manual labor less honorable than other forms of work? . . . What is the relationship of person, position, and wealth to law? . . . What is a woman? . . . How do you develop motivation, or group action, or a will to do? . . . How can you connect academic learning to practical living? . . . Are there springs in a man's nature of real concern over social ills, or other-interest rather than self-interest, of humane treatment of suffering animals? . . . How do you develop a conscience for truth, integrity, righteousness? . . . Will educated young people stay in their homes and villages and apply their education? . . . Whose are the natural resources of the earth? How ought we to care for them and use them?

These and many more are not academic questions. They are alive in men's hands out there on that mountain. They are the raw material that must be taken up and dealt with to make the New Nepal.

To work earnestly at questions of community improvement brings one sooner or later to the conviction that such improvement depends primarily on the character or disposition of the people. The springs of better things, when they flow, come from the hearts of men.

From "Nation Building—Fundamental Education" by Jonathan Lindell, in *Lutheran World*, Vol. VII, No. 4, March, 1961. Used by permission.

The frontiers for Christian mission are not solely geographical. They are cultural, political, social, scientific, economic. They are found in every area of human experience, and in each area Christians must seek to make the gospel known. A new and important frontier of the church is discussed by M. A. Z. Rolston, secretary for industrial services of the National Christian Council in India.

The Industrial World

India has been known for a long time as an agricultural country and as being under the strain of a rapidly increasing population. Ever since freedom was attained, she has set herself to the much needed task of economic transformation. Consequently rapid industrial growth is evident everywhere in the country. This is not only essential for raising the standard of living and for better economic opportunities for the growing population, but it is also extremely necessary, since without economic democracy our hard-earned freedom and political democracy will have only a very remote chance to survive. This does not mean that industry is absolutely new to the country but rather that the country is under rapid industrial expansion.

While we built industry as we could, prior to independence, that was absolutely insufficient and inadequate for our needs.

This accelerated industrialization is not only changing the Indian economic pattern but is also introducing social change. In the first place rapid industrialization is resulting in greater urbanization. Old industrial towns like Kanpur and Asansol are expanding, and new ones such as Sindri, Durgapur, Rourkela, and Bhilai, are replacing obscure villages. Further, urbanization and industrialization together have introduced the element of mobility in this tradition oriented society and have brought into existence an uprooted community.

The old industrial cities had slums that gradually took on a village-like character; they preserved the pre-industrial way of life. Now slum clearance and rehabilitation programs in these cities are tearing the people away from their accustomed neighborhoods, relocating them in newly built colonies on the outskirts of the cities where they are thrown with people of all kinds. Their resistance to adjustment forces on them anonymity and uprootedness.

When new cities spring up, people move to them from villages as well as from overcrowded cities. Thus a large number of people in these new situations are struggling against the disintegration of the family and the traditional social set-up. People must now seek new adjustments that will not be possible unless they discover things in common with others. There are other problems, too, in this uprooted community: leisure, organized social vices, corruption, demoralization, and class conflict.

In the old industrial centers the church was established long ago and usually in the heart of the city. The Christian community thronged around the various denominational churches. With improvements now coming to these cities the Christians, like others, are moving to the suburban colonies. Here they are cut off from their respective churches and are thrown together with members of different denominations with whom they do not freely associate. Unfortunately, the Christians mostly are an ingrown community and have not shown much interest in associating with others, nor do they show any such inclination now. The result is that they also have a sense of lostness in the new situation.

What is true of Christians as an ingrown community in the old industrial cities is also true of them in the new cities. Here again members of several denominations are thrown together who do not find free association easy. Besides, in the new industrial towns fellowship is difficult due to linguistic and cultural differences, since economic prospects have drawn Christians to these new cities from many parts of the country.

In both cases we find lack of fellowship and of a sense of belonging, absence of community feeling, loss of church and congregational life, loss of the educative influence of the church in the lives of migrant Christians, and indifference towards matters affecting citizenship.

The entire situation of social disorder presents an immense new frontier beckoning the church to reach and help people and give them direction for a better social order. The church has developed an erroneous notion that it can only help people who approach it for help. This same notion was the cause of indifference shown by the church to the industrial frontier in the West during and after the industrial revolution, with the tragic result that people came to regard the church as irrelevant in their daily life.

It is a matter of great satisfaction that the church in India is concerned that it does not repeat the mistake of the church in the West. It is really exciting to know that the church here is moving in a new direction and is discovering the industrial world as its parish and an area of concern. It is realizing that social sickness in the industrial world is aggravated by lack of an education that gives people the sense of being responsible for others, of belonging together. The church is realizing, though slowly, that men who spend their lives in the industrial mileu need to be taught that their good is altogether identified with the good of everyone else in society, and that understanding between the various interest groups is essential for peace and progress. The church is becoming more and more conscious of its duty to help people discover the common manhood essential to reducing the social distance between the various interest groups. It is really gratifying to note that the church is discovering that it has a tremendous responsibility and a unique opportunity to exercise its educative influence and ultimately its ministry of reconciliation.

The result of this new consciousness is a pioneer corps, "Christian Industrial Service," which sees its special purpose in terms of the following responsibilities:

1. *To promote "house churches."* House churches are initiated in industrial centers for those who were cut off from the church when they moved to suburban housing colonies.

2. *To promote churches in the new industrial cities.* These churches in the new cities and the house churches in the suburban colonies of old industrial cities are established on a union basis, to help Christians break down the denominational reserve and find fellowship in worship and Christian living with other Christians regardless of their affiliations and other differences. Here they are trained to feel that they are the church in a challenging situation, and that the church does not exist for itself but that Christ has commissioned its members to live for others. Here Christians are helped to discover through Bible study and discussion that the gospel has a message for the man living under

the shadows of industry. Here the laity in industry are trained and awakened to lead men to Christ, in whom we have the answer to all our problems. Christians and non-Christians are invited to worship services, Bible study groups, meetings, and festivals, and though the number who respond to the invitation is not large, it nevertheless brings encouragement and hope to all concerned.

3. *To organize institutes and conferences.* These are to train workers and leaders in the church to serve the industrial community. Consciousness of responsibility is different from the knowledge of what one should do, and both are required of a Christian to make him a useful member of the church, community, and society. Christian Industrial Service organizes conferences and institutes wherein specialists in industrial evangelism, church leaders, pastors, and laymen working in industry get together to study industrial and urban problems, share experiences and views, and consider how best a Christian can grapple with, and help others grapple with, those problems. Here also we consider how aware the Christians are of the requirements of citizenship such as voting in elections or membership in political parties and trades unions, and the like. Also people are helped here to make an intelligent study of their Christian responsibilities in these vital areas of decision.

4. *To educate the industrial community in responsible citizenship.* A very large percentage of industrial workers in India are illiterate and of low intellectual caliber, with hardly any sense of values . . . they lack education almost completely. Through personal work among them, through audio-visual aids wherever possible, and through literature for those who can read, the workers are being helped to recognize in trade unions their natural community and the agency of social control. They are also being helped through these efforts to lead a more useful life mentally,

spiritually, and socially and to appreciate that their well-being is totally identified with the well-being of the society.

5. *To prepare and publish adequate literature for the education of the industrial community.* Only a very modest beginning has been made in this direction so far. A monthly bulletin, *Christian Industrial Service,* has been published since December, 1959. It carries news of the various Christian centers in industrial towns and views on matters of importance to an industrial community. Since adequate literature relevant to the Indian industrial situation is sadly lacking, a regular editorial board has been set up to prepare and publish suitable material.

It will not be out of place to mention that industrial evangelism views with concern the problem of unemployment. Unemployment saps the very humanity in man, gives him a feeling of futility and of being a social castaway, and in his bitterness turns him into an antagonist of society. Industrial evangelism cannot create employment, nor can it at this stage help people to qualify to compete for employment. Yet through conferences, institutes, and literature, a constant campaign is being waged to make the church more conscious of the fact that man's living is the church's concern, too, and that the church must do all it can to help people better their prospects of securing employment. Emphasis is being laid on programs and projects for training youth in technology to prepare them for competition and hard work.

The rootlessness of the industrial community is another very important problem. Thousands of people were drawn into the new industrial towns a few years ago to help on construction jobs. They struggled hard to put their roots down. Now that most of the construction in the cities is nearing completion, the families are facing unemployment and homelessness. Because of their poverty, they find it hard to go back to their villages. The situation is becoming increasingly serious and perplexing to the government. Although the church may not be able to do very much to meet the problem, Christians have a responsibility to be informed about it and to play a role in developing a program of public assistance.

Christian Industrial Service is a church agency that is still in its infancy. Its efforts are humble and its results are far from startling. Yet it inspires hope in all associated with it and interested in it.

Adapted from the article by Mr. Rolston in *World Christian Education*, Third Quarter, 1960. Used by permission.

Christianity meets three other world faiths, Hinduism, Buddhism, and Islam, in Southern Asia. It also encounters animism, the mixture of fear, superstition, and religion that makes up primitive peoples' belief in spirit beings.

Assam is a state in northeast India where faith in Jesus Christ has captured the hearts of thousands of former animists. The growth of the church there is described by Wilfred Scopes. Dr. Scopes, a missionary in Southern Asia for a number of years, is now an executive of the Division of World Mission and Evangelism, the World Council of Churches.

Assam: Youngest of All

The significance of Assam in the Christian enterprise is not as generally recognized as it deserves to be. There has been a lack of publicity. For one thing the area is isolated from the main stream of Indian life; for another, during British rule, few missionary societies were allowed to operate. Apart from the Church of England, whose priests ministered almost exclusively to British personnel in government employ or on tea estates, the only other churches sponsoring mission work were American and British Baptists and the Welsh Presbyterians. All others were denied entry until Indian independence. The first permanent mission in Assam was in fact established by a pioneer named Nathan Brown, of the American Baptist Mission, who

began work among the Ao Nagas at Sadiya in 1836. It has pros-
pered and spread beyond all human expectations. English Baptists have churches of comparable basic strength in more limited
areas, notably South Lushai. Their work has been supplemented
among other tribes by Baptists from Australia and New Zealand.
There are newer and more conservative groups coming now
from America, some of which are Baptist. Thus if Kerala is
noted for "coconuts, bishops and ducks," Assam may be said to
be noted for "tea, bamboo and Baptists."

Assam is India in miniature. There are between forty and
fifty-five languages spoken there. Along the northern border of
the state run the foothills of the Himalayas, where many tribes
dwell, many of them unknown and as yet unreached by the gospel: Abors, Opatanis, Miris, and several Naga tribes.

In the valley of the mighty Brahmaputra River live the Assamese people, who compose the largest single group within the
state. They are mostly Hindus and Muslims. The economy of
the valley depends largely on the cultivation of tea, which calls
for imported labor from as far as South India.

The Garo Hills lie in the southwest corner of Assam. The
Garos, like all the tribal people, are virile, independent, and
hard working, and were originally animists with comparatively
high moral and ethical standards. About 50 per cent of the
population is now Christian. Adjacent to the Garo Hills lie the
beautiful Khasi and Jaintia Hills, where dwell the lovable, singing Khasis, of whom about 50 per cent are also Christians. Next
are the North Cachar and Mikir Hills, where many small tribes
live with their own languages and social patterns, and about 40
per cent are Christian.

Running north and south are the famed Naga Hills, where
Lhotos, Aos, Semas, Angamis, and other tribes dwell. About 75
per cent of these are Christian. In recent years there have been

serious political disturbances. At one time it was thought by the
government that missionaries were abetting the rebels, but the
charge now seems to be dropped. The fact is that independent
hill folk have objected to being governed by the Assamese plains
folk. Hopeful signs are not wanting that some settlement is in
sight. One of them has been the establishing of Nagaland as a
state.

It is reported that on the occasion of a visit a few years ago,
Mr. Nehru rebuked a Baptist pastor for visiting the rebels. The
reply was given with simple dignity, "Should I not as a father
seek to bring back an erring son?" That particular pastor frankly
expected to lose his life in his constant coming and going between those in the rebel camp and those supporting the government. But he was quite unafraid.

Along the Burma border, and next to Nagaland, lies the state
of Manipur, where in the hills are to be found again many different tribes. Christian work in this state has been restricted by
government officials. West of Manipur is the district of Cachar
where small groups of tribesmen live among a majority population of Bengalis. A strong Christian church is found in the area
south of Cachar known as the Lushai (Mizo) Hills. The northern part has been evangelized by the Welsh Presbyterians and
the south by the English Baptists. Relations are such that there
is an interchange of membership and maximum co-operation.
But it is hard for people who do not live in those parts to realize
how difficult is the problem of communication among the in-
accessible hills. It often takes ten days to send a letter one hundred miles. The story of Christian work in North Lushai has
been written by the Rev. J. M. Lloyd in a little book called *On
Every High Hill.* It is a testimony to the transforming power of
the gospel that a people who just over sixty years ago were
famous as head hunters are now famous for their literacy, the

rate ranging from 90 to 95 per cent. The initial work of evangelism in that area is now completed and the church numbers 113,000. These people support entirely the ministry and the Aijal Theological Seminary; they also contribute to the educational and medical work. There is a printing press and its most popular products are Bible commentaries!

In 1956 I visited Cherrapunji in the Khasi Hills, which long held the doubtful distinction of being the wettest place in the world. In the early British days it was the capital of Assam. The change-over to Shillong was made in 1864, one factor being the poor morale of the British garrison who, in spite of their upbringing in Great Britain, found the incessant rain of Cherrapunji intolerable! A severe earthquake in 1897 brought down most of the buildings in the town, but today it looks fairly prosperous if a little damp, and there is a theological seminary that serves all areas of the United Church in Assam and maintains a high standard of training for a rural ministry.

The Eastern Theological College, Jorhat, which like the Cherrapunji institution is affiliated to Serampore University for purposes of diplomas and degrees, mainly serves a Baptist constituency from the Naga Hills. It has a fine plant and is seeking to strengthen its staff with a view to offering the Serampore B.D. course. There are also no less than eighteen Bible schools for the training of leaders—mostly laymen—largely supported by their individual churches over short periods of three months or so. The Protestant church in Assam, which claims a constituency of at least one million persons, is growing and expanding at a phenomenal rate.

A colleague of mine recently attended a Baptist convention where five thousand delegates were present. In the two villages located near the site of the convention the people took very seriously their role as hosts. Each family provided a pig, a bundle of firewood, a bundle of hay for the covering of the temporary pavilion, and one bag of rice out of every fifteen bags in their possession. At the convention a report was given of a considerable increase in church membership. Some recent converts from another area referred to the persecution on the part of their neighbors and it was suggested that perhaps a policy of concentration and consolidation might be wise. To which came the reply, "But they come to our meetings and decide they want to be Christians, and then they go home and tell their people and they decide they want to be Christians. And we can't stop them!"

The Indian field secretary of the American Baptists recently visited the Konyak tribe along the Burma border and heard a report from the local minister about evangelistic advance. The latter concluded, "We are marching toward Burma, and we shall not stop until we meet the evangelists coming from the other side."

Is there any wonder that those of us who are privileged to visit Assam should be thrilled and impressed by this youngest of all the churches in India? If we ask why is it that such sweeping advance is possible in Assam and not in the rest of India, we must readily admit in human terms that in the absence of the challenge of forms of religion higher than animism, as well as the absence of caste distinctions, hill people more readily respond to the Christian message. The strength of the Assam church is seen in its laity, who have always constituted the spearhead of evangelism. What is now needed is top leadership to widen horizons and lead the church wisely in these days of opportunity. Steps have been taken and are being taken by Serampore College as well as the National Christian Council to help meet this need.

From *Indian Opportunity*, by Wilfred Scopes, with adaptations by the author. Published by The Edinburgh House Press, London, 1961. Used by permission.

*To be a Christian in Southern Asia means to live with the tensions
that are felt by minority groups. To be a young person, particularly a
student, is to be caught up in the tug of war between old and new.
The Christian youth of Pakistan exist in both conditions. A report of
their experience is given by Miriam McGaw Benade, a former missionary there.*

Pakistan: Great Expectations

One day in 1947, two weeks after Pakistan had become a
free and independent nation, a group of handsome young fron-
tiersmen boarded a train at Rawalpindi. Although they carried
picturesque homemade firearms, they were obviously in a cele-
brating mood. When someone asked them about their tickets,
they answered gaily that they didn't have any: "Pakistan has
been made. We are Pakistanis. This train is ours. Why should
we pay for a ride on something that belongs to us?"

Fifteen years have passed, years of both chaos and exultation
for Pakistan, and her young people have learned that national
independence is a matter of serious responsibility as well as pride.

Probably the most thoughtful of these young people are the

students. An inquiry was made recently of Pakistani students and of the adults who know them intimately. The gist of the inquiry was this: "What is it like to be a student—and in particular a Christian student—in Pakistan today?" The responses are important not only for what they reveal about youth but also for what they imply for Pakistan and the life of the church there.

A Pakistani who is a professor of history said that his students are impatient because political stability and economic and social changes are coming too slowly. He has found pessimism and lack of purpose widespread among them.

An American working in Pakistan gave a different appraisal:

"The people of this country are painfully and slowly divesting themselves of a sense of weakness and inferiority. There is enough faith and idealism to make young people believe that an Islamic constitution will usher in a new age. Yet there is enough realism to recognize that only by hard work and achievement in performance can Pakistan prosper. The thoughtful student sees this, although the translation of this insight into political and social action remains to be done."

The comment of another history teacher needs to be framed by the warmth of her personality. She is a small person, but her dark eyes glow with intense feeling when she speaks of Pakistan. A teacher in a girls' college in Lahore, she is a dedicated Muslim. Her mind is informed by wide reading, and her analysis of student attitudes has a broad perspective:

"The breath-taking progress of science and the great material benefits that mankind has enjoyed as a result of it have had a deep impact on the thought of man. His sense of values, standards of judgement, and purpose of existence have been guided by a materialistic philosophy of life. For a time, acquisition of material ends and benefits proved enough of an incentive and justification for existence. However, this very accomplishment challenges him relentlessly with a gigantic question—what next? "It is at this point that materialistic philosophy stands discredited. Man finds his life hollow and meaningless. He begins to indulge in escapism. This has manifested itself in the 'Beat Generation' of America and the 'Angry Young Men' of England.

"This failure of materialistic philosophy in America and Europe has its counterpart in Pakistan, the difference being the time factor only. The question, 'What next?' has not yet been encountered by young students and graduates, but the problem does exist and may carry them to its logical conclusion, if something is not done to arrest the condition.

"For a student community, immersed in a materialistic attitude toward life and finding no way out, wondering why man exists and getting no answer, there are very few possibilities for an optimistic attitude."

Pakistan was born as an independent republic in 1947 when the British-ruled subcontinent of India was divided into two nations. Pakistan was created as a Muslim nation and India as one that was primarily Hindu. The autumn of 1947 was a time when Hindu and Muslim communities moved from one country to another, the Hindus hastening to India and the Muslims fleeing to Pakistan. Bitterness between the two groups flamed into violence and both new nations were shaken by the slaughter and destruction that resulted. In those days, fresh memories of flight, death, and fear haunted college dormitories and classrooms.

Today Pakistan is the largest Muslim nation in the world, with a population of some 94 million. The problems of establishing a firm nationhood are gradually being overcome. A small core of dedicated leaders is working hard toward establishing a basic democracy, stabilizing the economy, opening new highways, and broadening educational programs.

A young Christian Pakistani has observed that "the emergence of this new and largest of Islamic states gives the Muslim a sense of liberation after centuries of political decay, impotence, and subjection; and infuses him with tremendous exaltation."

On the other hand, development of a modern state frequently conflicts with old practices and attitudes, and the contest beween old and new bewilders and disturbs Pakistan's youth.

Colleges and schools are filled with a new generation of students who have not suffered the harsh experiences of their older brothers and sisters. But in their own way they are involved in the adjustments and hazards of nation-building. They have inherited all the problems of prepartition India and, because of the swift flow of world events, they also face new dilemmas. They are wrestling with the meanings of cyclotrons, space travel, the Kinsey reports, and Western films while they study English texts on economics, political science, and the physical sciences.

These interests compete with natural Pakistani pride in the great days of Islamic conquests in Asia, Africa, and Europe; and in scientific and philosophic studies made by Muslim savants when most European scholarship was sleeping.

But pride in Islamic achievement has not quite obliterated the sense of inferiority that poisoned Islamic thinking because of the minority position of Muslims in the old, undivided India. And though Westerners—especially Americans—are frequently suspected of holding condescending attitudes, there is a dream in the heart of almost every young Pakistani student that one day he will visit the West and study in a Western university and even learn how to earn "big money."

Economic problems and the fear of joblessness haunt Pakistan's youth. They are bewildered by the changes taking place; some are angered by them, others are impatient that the changes come so slowly. The stuff of living and thinking is in their hands. Out of it they must fashion their values. Will love of money, pride of position, envy, and jealousy control their attitudes, or will there be room in their thinking for self-respect, integrity, service to fellowmen, and reverence for God?

Against this general background of feeling, several divergent patterns appear. An American professor classified Pakistani students into three major groups:

A vociferous minority of ultraconservatives who seek a return to past practices and interpretations of their sacred book, the Qur'an. These have been most vocal in recent months and join in making an outcry against Christian institutions.

A majority middle group that represents all shades of social, religious, and economic opinion, and in general takes a middle position between conservatives and liberals. Those who are indifferent or apathetic might also be listed here. Recently, disgusted with the old fashioned views of the president of the University Students Union, the majority group threw him out. All is not apathy among them!

The third group, the modern or westernized group, is relatively smaller in number. Here are those who wish to westernize most of their habits and cultural interests. Here are others who are more concerned with political modifications and those who favor rapid socioeconomic changes.

Conflicting opinions swirl around young university women. They are entering various professions, especially teaching and medicine. Some become enamored with wealth and selfish show, but many more are thoughtful wives and mothers and leaders of wholesome social effort in their communities. However, a young engineer voiced his doubts about Pakistan's women in these words:

"The so-called purdah-observing women [those who customarily would not appear in mixed groups of men and women except in their own immediate families] have thrown off their veils and are out to compete with men in every sphere. They are even trying to gain admission to engineering colleges. They are fighting hard to get their equal share in every walk of life. They have developed their fashions to an extreme. Seeing this trend, one wonders if these are the nation's mothers! What culture gave them no desire to be mothers, but instead to become decoration pieces?"

Another point of tension that troubles some Pakistani young people is what one person has called a "split in the social environment." It is a "dangerous gulf separating the intelligentsia from the common man." The educated man is exasperated with the common man's traditional attitudes. He fears that such attitudes may ensnare not only the man who holds them but the whole nation in helpless poverty. Thus the nation will be prevented from taking its rightful place in international life.

Religion is moderately interesting to Pakistani youth. In general, their attitudes are quite like those of students in almost any other country, and just as varied:

"Students believe that religion is an important factor that gives moral background and controls life."

"Some students give lip service to religion only because of social pressure."

"A few are almost completely disinterested except for social and cultural implications regarding such matters as marriage practices."

"When occasion arises, the student will passionately champion the cause of Islam."

"It is a great pity that we are going away and away from our own religion. Partly it is due to our religious leaders who indulge in politics. I am personally convinced of the truth of Islam, but I do not believe that Islam has a monopoly of truth. I have special respect for the Christian faith. I also respect the faith and doctrines of other people."

The history teacher from Lahore who was quoted earlier in

this article is particularly interested in religion. She feels that in general students and young graduates are not only indifferent but skeptical about the authority vested in religious leaders and about traditional religion. She said:

"Students may not openly speak out their doubts or criticize anything that has religious sanction but their silence should not be mistaken for acceptance of traditional religion. Traditional religion cannot satisfy. Students have entered the age of mental maturity; they demand conviction, not blind, unquestioning obedience.

"Religion that is merely a personal affair, religion that stands in the way of political, economic, and social progress, religion that is nothing but a sum total of superstitions—such religion cannot stand the challenge of life and therefore cannot be acceptable to youth.

"Yet youth is conscious that there are certain values in life that are permanent, values that give a foothold in the ever-changing world, a changelessness in change. If there are any permanent values, they must pervade the entire life."

This woman is a member of a new movement "for spreading the teachings of the Holy Qur'an amongst the intelligentsia in the light of modern knowledge in a rational way." She feels that the movement, Tolu-E-Islam, will capture the minds and imaginations of the intelligentsia and will be instrumental in helping them to find "permanent values, the source of which is the Qur'an." Here they will discover that "God is neither merciful nor revengeful, he is the Just Law Giver."

As Muslims were a minority group in old India, so Christians are a very small minority in Pakistan. Their number totals about 733,000. Certain groups in the country are disturbed by the "phenomenal growth" of the Christian population that was revealed by the recent census. But in spite of some fanatical opposition, the Christian church in Pakistan is slowly lengthening its cords and strengthening its stakes. Leading Protestant denominations are negotiating to establish a United Church of Pakistan. Already they co-operate in the proceedings of the West Pakistan Christian Council. Christian leaders in Pakistan like Dr. Andrew Thakur Das and Bishop Chandu Ray are well known in ecumenical circles.

One strong Christian influence is the work of the five Christian colleges in West Pakistan. Kinnaird College is exclusively for women; Gordon and Murray Colleges have co-educational programs; Edwards and Forman Colleges serve men students. These colleges are attended in large numbers by Muslims, but each institution has a small, growing nucleus of Christian students. In colleges and schools, in rural and urban areas, Muslims and Christians have opportunity to work and play together. This kind of experience is the best possible one for breaking down barriers and prejudices.

Difficult adjustments face young Christians coming to colleges from rural communities. An increasing number each year emerges from poverty-stricken environments to attend school. Here they come in contact with Muslim students, many of whom are from homes of wealth and culture. The Muslims are inclined to look down on Christians as outcasts in the first place and secondly as "stool pigeons of Western imperialists." A considerable number of Christians receive scholarship aid that frequently is insufficient to let them live on the same scale as other students. They often must improve their study habits and learn to compete in scholastic fields. They have to discover their talents in athletics, music, and drama, and exercise them in order to win the approval and acceptance of their fellows. In every sense they are faced with the problems of "getting along" in a new environment. Even more, they must re-examine the Christian values that heretofore they have accepted almost unques-tioningly. In every university situation, young Christians are called upon to examine, purify, strengthen, and enrich their beliefs and ideals, and to share them intelligently and with dig-nity with those who have other points of view. Somehow, con-sciousness of membership in a despised minority group must not deter the growth of the personalities and characters of young Christians. They must grow—in favor with God and man.

A comment on these problems was made by a young Pakistani who was a student at Forman College and is today working to-ward a doctor of philosophy degree in an American university. His family had been Christians for just three years when he was born. Before coming to the United States for postgraduate stud-ies, he was associate secretary of the Student Christian Move-ment in Pakistan. His ideas regarding the role of the Christian community in Pakistan and the problems of Christian students were expressed in these words:

"The Christian student in Pakistan lives in a nation whose government has consciously aimed to establish the Islamic way of life. The Christian student is part of two worlds. As a citizen he is part of a Muslim state, as a Christian he is part of the church. Islam, like some Christian churches, has not always furthered liberty of conscience. This creates a problem for an honest Christian student.

"The church is a tiny minority. And as we look at ourselves, we cannot run away from what the majority of Muslims assert—that the Christian faith is still inexcapably related with the West.

"Also it is haunted by minority attitudes of always feeling discriminated against, always being persecuted. This attitude has made the church an exclusive community. From this community a Christian student goes into the life of his nation. But he re-mains a foreigner in it. He does not seem to get out of his minority complexes and does not use opportunities for presenting Christ to Muslims.

"These problems present a tremendous challenge, calling for active engagement with Muslim associates in a spirit of honesty and forthrightness."

This young man realizes the "limitations of career opportunities" in his country, especially for Christians. However he believes Christians should choose vocations that will lead into "the main stream of the nation." He said that Christians must take part in all aspects of the life of the nation and must seek to be rid of foreignness that isolates them from Muslim Pakistanis.

Speaking of religious discussions between Christians and Muslims, he said that Christians should act, not boastfully about their faith, "but as ones who call people to share the experiences that we have had in Christ. At the same time it also means listening to Muslims tell their religious experience and thus engage in a dialogue.

"I believe that a Christian student can best make a contribution to the life of the university by consciously living as a Christian who respects what Islam has to offer. We must meet Muslims in the presence of God under whose judgement we stand."

Constitutionally, Christians in Pakistan have all the rights of free citizens in a republic, but in a variety of ways discrimination against them is sometimes shown as "a sort of subtle persecution." This situation calls for insight and patience as well as courage on the part of the Christian community. Christian conviction free from fanaticism, devotion to high principles and to national progress will in time do much to win the regard of the Muslim majority in the country. Pakistani Christian homes, schools, and churches need to learn appreciation of the fine aspects of national culture even as they also learn to emphasize good citizenship and Christian ideals of daily living.

John McKay, former president of Princeton Seminary, once said that it is the business of Christians to identify themselves with the best in the environment where they live and serve. Only then do they win the right to be heard. Thoughtful Christians in Pakistan increasingly realize the full implications of the sort of identification of which McKay spoke—that of finding common ground and friendship even with those who profess certain ideas and beliefs different from their own.

At Christian colleges, Muslims and Christians learn to appreciate one another and work together. Here they receive the inspiration of selflessness and of service to their nation. They share ennobling loyalty to the ideals of their institutions. Graduates of Forman College never forget the college motto: "By love serve one another."

Within the church, young Christians are seeking to convince older leaders of their desire "actively to participate" in the life of the church and assume responsibilities for carrying on its program.

One of them said that "the young student needs the church, as the church needs him." Such leadership must be recognized and encouraged. When young Christians have questions and doubts, when they frankly speak their minds "in humility and earnestness," the older members in the church "should be willing to accept the earnest of their doubts and create conditions whereby doubts can be met with honesty." The young man continued:

"The Christian student faces a tremendous challenge, both from Pakistan as a nation and the Christian church. He is not required to consider them as compartmentalized areas of responsibility, but as one and the same. He is called to be a Christian in both these areas of life. He must be a visible symbol of Christian presence among Muslim associates. He must recognize his responsibility to the new social, economic, and political life of his nation. He must be part of the world that God loves. Pakistan is a field for spiritual and mental growth, demanding intelligence, imagination, and will. This is a challenge indeed, which is both problem and opportunity."

"*I must be His minister*"

Southern Asia's churches have nurtured outstanding leaders. Augustine Ralla Ram of India was one. The son of a pastor from the Punjab, he became a leader of the World Student Christian Federation, the International Missionary Council, and the World Council of Churches. From young manhood, he worked passionately for church union. When he died in 1957 at fifty-eight years of age, he was planning a meeting on church union in northern India.

Ralla Ram did not come to the ministry easily. This description of his call is from his biography, I Must Speak, by Myra Scovel. It also shows the part his parents played in determining his vocation, a role that may seem strange to some Westerners. To Asian Christians, the Bible provides good support for such a relationship between parents and son. Many an Indian pastor was first set apart for the ministry by his father and mother.

Augustine Ralla Ram

The rains had broken in the old Punjab city of Lahore and the young man leaving the gates of Rang Mahal School loved the rains. He lifted his face to the sky. Tomorrow he would be going home! No more trying to keep these students out of mischief by an agile rendition of Shakespeare; no more trying to combat Morpheus with Milton—at least not until the autumn term.

But would he be coming back to his job as teacher? He was on his way now to his beloved Forman Christian College to collect the things he had left there. Would he be seeing his old school again when the seasons changed?

He stopped under a lamp post to wipe the rain from his face.

55

College had been fun all the way through and the year of teaching at Rang Mahal had been a good one. He liked sharing his love for English literature with his fellow-Punjabis. It would be a good life in the academic atmosphere that meant so much to him. He would have time to read and read and read. His mental capacities would grow and develop here. But the still, small Voice kept breaking into his complacency. One day he would have to settle with that Voice.

Footsteps echoed down the hollow street; foreign shoe leather, not the clip-clop of Punjabi slippers. A figure appeared in the far circle of light.

"Ah, Dr. Velte, good evening, sir," said the young man.

"Good evening, Augustine. I have been wanting to have a talk with you. What do you plan to do after the holidays?"

"Why, come back here, I suppose, sir," said Augustine Ralla Ram.

"No, Augustine. It will not do. Your father and your mother dedicated you for the ministry. You must come to grips with God's plan for your life. Why not come to Saharanpur and prepare yourself for the ministry of God's word to your people? Think about it, pray about it, talk it over with your father while you are at home in Jullundur and I will see you at Saharanpur at the beginning of the term. Good night, Augustine."

The young man walked on in the rain. What Dr. Velte had said was true; his parents had dedicated him, their first-born, to the ministry. But could he not serve God in any other way than by being a padre? He had not neglected his service for Christ even during his school days. From his earliest years in the Christian Boys' School in Ludhiana, he had given himself so diligently to the study of the Bible that twice he had gained distinction by standing first in the Punjab and had received the Lake Memorial History Prize in Bible examination. What unhappy years they had been, those first years after his mother's death, when his father, not knowing what to do with his three active sons, had sent them away to boarding school!

And here in Lahore, he had been secretary and treasurer of the Christian Endeavor Society; he had gone regularly with his professors to preach in Anarkali Bazar; he had attended YMCA camps; he had held prayer meetings in the homes of the poor; he had been active in leading devotions at the student prayer meetings. He smiled to himself as he recalled that, as a penalty for one of his many misdeeds, a teacher had punished him in the one way that would touch him most deeply—he had not been allowed to offer prayer at the weekly student prayer meeting!

Ah, those pranks! And the plays—what a pleasure it had been to be a student, to act the part of Brutus in *Julius Caesar:*

"Not that I loved Caesar less but that I loved Rome more. Had you rather Caesar were living and die all slaves, than that Caesar were dead to live all free men?"

That had been a great night. And the coffers of the National Missionary Society had been better filled as a result. There had been many another entertainment or variety show which he had organized to raise money for this cause so close to his heart. He hummed one of the songs that the boys were always asking him to sing—

> "Sahib jawe Kalcutta,
>
> Memsahib jawe Kalcutti
>
> Aur ham bechara Khalasi . . ."

> (The Sahib has gone to Calcutta,
>
> The Memsahib's gone to Calcutti
>
> And I, poor soul, am left alone . . .)

He entered the college grounds, glancing up at the sign: FORMAN CHRISTIAN COLLEGE. He owed a lot to this institution, to its professors, to Dr. J. C. R. Ewing himself. Some of the boys had been afraid of their principal. Augustine wondered why. He remembered how shocked one of the young professors had been the day he had dared to disagree with the venerable man. What was the issue? No matter, he, Augustine, had had the temerity to say, "But, Sir, I disagree with you."

Gruffly, Dr. Ewing had replied, "Young man, you are not to speak to me like that."

"But again I venture to say, Sir, that I do not agree with you," Augustine had replied.

Perhaps the young professor had not caught the twinkle in Dr. Ewing's eye as Augustine had when the two went on with their discussion. Not that it would have mattered if Dr. Ewing had been truly perturbed; the young student standing before him felt it his moral duty to speak out when he disagreed.

But all these reminiscences were not helping Augustine Ralla Ram to solve his problem. He knew very well what Dr. Ewing would want him to do; what his father would want him to do. Was he willing to walk the stony path that his father was now walking? A padre was so at the mercy of his parishioners.

"I haven't the patience," he said to himself. But the still, small Voice persisted and the pressure of an unseen Hand was upon his shoulder. Going into Kennedy Hall to pick up his belongings, he felt he was looking at things for the last time.

•   •   •

Father and son were drinking their morning tea on the veranda of their home, the pastor's residence in Jullundur. Leaf shadows played upon the red brick wall of the Golak Nath Memorial Church nearby.

"You've been back with us to our ancestral village many times,

Augustine," said the older man. "You know the church in Ghore-waha; you know the history of it and that our beloved Kali Charan Chatterji baptized me there. All this, your background, has bearing on what led up to your decision last night to become a minister of the Lord Jesus Christ. From September first, 1888, the day you were born, until this very morning, I have never ceased from praying daily that you would be led by God to take this step. It takes me back to the days when I had to take my stand for Christ."

"Tell me the story again, Papa," said Augustine, knowing how his father loved to tell it.

"I have often wondered why Kali Charan Chatterji chose our village of Ghorewaha as his place of preaching. There must have been a hundred other villages in the district," said Padre Ralla Ram, shifting his tall, emaciated frame in the wooden, slat-back chair. "Such a small village it is, far from the main road, a com-bination of Rajput Muslims and Hindus as inhabitants. We Hindus were certainly in the minority and ours one of the very few Brahmin families. Your grandparents were very devout peo-ple, Augustine. Being an only son, I was loved and cherished by them in a special way.

"They gave me the name, 'Ralla Ram,'—'Mixed with God,' 'Thrown into the stream with God.' I was taught how to fulfill my religious duties; daily I went to the temple with my father. When we got home, all the dogs in the village would be at our door waiting for me to feed them. Then I would go up on the roof and feed the birds. Gradually I left the things of the world, and though a young man, I spent most of the hours of the day meditating and praying.

"At about this time, I learned that a Bengali from Calcutta was in the village preaching a new doctrine. I sought him out and heard from the lips of Kali Charan Chatterji the story of how God so loved the world that He gave His only Son that whoever believed in Him should not perish but have eternal life. I heard the call, 'Come to me, all who labor and are heavy-laden, and I will give you rest.' Such thoughts were like a cool hand on my forehead. For hours I read the New Testament, hiding the Gospel portions under the floor lest my father find them.

"At about this time my father died and out of deference to him and because of my love for him, I gave myself up to fulfilling the Hindu rites prescribed for his mourning. But the words of Jesus kept coming back to me: 'Whosoever shall deny me before men, him will I also deny before my Father which is in heaven.' At last the day came when I could no longer face the deceptive life I was leading and I asked for baptism.

"I will never forget the tearing of my heart as I stood at the front of the church hearing my mother wail as she stood in the doorway. The hostile crowd surrounding the church building meant nothing to me but when my mother fell in a swoon, cutting her head on the stone floor till the blood gushed forth, my love cried out to her. Our friends and relatives carried her away. I stood where I was without the power to move a foot, seeming to know that the thing I was about to do was the only right one. I received the sacrament of baptism. Amid all the persecution that followed and even with all my heartaches as pastor, I have never for one moment regretted it. And you know, Son, how God did not leave it at that and what a joy it was to me when my aged mother received the same sacrament from these hands.

"The rest of the story you have heard many times—how I was turned out from my home and village, how Dr. Chatterji sent me to Saharanpur to study theology. Now you will be going to that same seminary. Your mother would be very happy, Augustine."

"What is this? Augustine going to seminary!" Annie, the sister and youngest member of the family came out of the house with their breakfast tray in her hands. "Oh, Tina Brother, I always knew you would be a padre."

"And how did you know that, little prophetess?" asked her brother.

"Oh, you were always preaching when we were children. Don't you remember how you would put one table on top of another to make a pulpit?"

"I remembered how, when I would be praying aloud, Julian would quietly overturn every chair that I had arranged as a 'congregation.' How angry little Philip would get!"

"But when Philip would tell you to beat Julian and you could very well have done so being the eldest, you would say, 'No, we must forgive him.' And right away you would start preaching a sermon on forgiveness."

"Run along, you two with your reminiscenses," said their father. "I must do some preparing before I go into the bazar to preach."

The two moved off under the trees.

"Oh Annie Bua, am I doing the right thing?" Augustine asked his sister. "I can preach, of that I have no fears. But will I be a good pastor? I get so impatient with people's stupidities and I fling out at them exactly what I think."

"Yes, Augustine, your tongue is too quick and too peppery but your heart is kind and that is what counts."

"God will have a hard time with me, Bua, but the path is clear. I must be His minister. Woe unto me if I preach not Christ."

Adapted from *I Must Speak*, by Myra Scovel. Published by The North India Christian Literature Society, Allahabad, 1961. Used by permission.

One of Augustine Ralla Ram's contributions was this poem:

A PRAYER FOR INDIA

We intercede before Thee for beloved Hindustan
    and our prayer is the same
    as that of ancient seekers after thee,
"From darkness lead us to light
    and from shadows to reality."
Mercifully grant that millions of this land
    forever engaged in arduous pilgrimages
    in search of peace and satisfaction
    may at last lay down their weary burdens
    at the feet of him who gives rest and peace
    to all those who labor and are heavy laden.
May they come at last to the haven of peace,
    even Jesus Christ,
    and find in him thine own response
    to their age-long quest.
To that end the frankincense of India's meditation,
    the myrrh of its renunciation and sacrifice,
    and the gold of its devotion
    be laid at the feet of Jesus Christ
    and may he be crowned Lord of all.

From *In His Name*, by George Appleton. Published by Macmillan & Company Ltd., London, and St. Martin's Press, New York, 1956. Used by permission.

The impact of Christianity on the status of women and the care of the sick is caught in this brief biographical sketch of a dedicated woman doctor by Elizabeth Meredith Lee.

Deena Sonna

The train from Bombay to Hyderabad came to a slow stop at a midway station. In one of the carriages sat a quiet-looking woman of India, lost in thought. She was reviewing the past two busy years of study in America, and thinking ahead to the challenge of the return to her own country. Suddenly the door of her compartment opened. Friends who had come half of her journey to meet her pelted her with fragrant garlands and offered food, in the Indian way of welcome. "Hurry and take your baggage," they urged her. "You must leave the train for we have come to meet you with the jeep. We will escort you home!"

As she drove through the countryside, the young woman's heart was full. She talked merrily with her friends, asking them about their children and their homes. As the jeep neared the village of Yellari, the traveler was told to get out of the conveyance. Now suddenly she was surrounded, not by a few friends, but a mass of people who formed a procession. Two bands led a thousand villagers, all cheering, singing, vying to place flowers around the neck of the homecomer. Not only from Yellari but also from many distant villages all over that area, these admirers had gathered, dressed in their colorful best, and with their arms heaped with garlands. They would greet a Christian woman who, to these villagers, was like a queen! And they told her right away that they had a surprise for her—a new well of cool, sweet water!

Behind this unique welcome lies the story of a young girl of India, brought up in a Christian home, for her father was a Methodist minister. How had she become the idol of a thousand village folk?

When she was five, little Deena Sonna was sent to a Christian boarding school. In time she became one of the first graduates of the Vanita Vidyalaya High School in Belgaum, where she taught for two years.

In choosing her vocation, Deena was influenced by her father. He was known as a Christian "medicine man," one who gives nature medicines to heal the sick of his parish. And he always accompanied his treatment with prayer. He wanted his child to be a doctor, and he was proud when she finally graduated from the four-year course at Vellore Christian Medical College, earning the degree of L.M.P.—Licensed Medical Practitioner—which the British law in India then recognized.

Deena's college days were rich not only in scientific learning but also in human relations and in Christian ideals. At Vellore she watched Dr. Ida Scudder and her associates as they led their students far beyond the realm of science, nurturing them carefully in the things of the spirit of Christ. With a deep-rooted resolve of service to humanity in her mind, it was not strange that young Dr. Deena Sonna declined high-salaried positions in secular institutions. She volunteered to go to a mission hospital, Ellen Cowen Memorial Hospital in Kolar, where she interned for one year and served four more as resident physician. The salary was low, but the opportunity to lead some of her fellow countrymen to Christ was as wide as the skies above her.

Deena's bent was for public health. She seized every opportunity to gain practical knowledge in this field. At different times she took leave of absence, six months to study and practice in the Health Department of the State of Mysore; another period for study in a rural health center established by the Rockefeller Foundation; another one in the Vaccine Institute. Always she was preparing herself for some service still undetermined.

Then one day this young physician knew where she wanted to put her life. There was an opportunity to start a public health experimental station under the auspices of The Methodist Church, of which she was a member. To get out into the Indian villages had been her dream; to heal the diseases so prevalent in the countryside and to teach people how to keep well was exactly what she most wanted to do.

One day in 1943 an old bullock cart jogged along the dusty road toward the village of Yellari, eighteen miles from a railroad and four miles from a main highway. Two young women rode in the cart, a woman of India and her companion, an American missionary. These friends, doctor and nurse, had been appointed to establish the Linn Dispensary and Health Center in Yellari, one of the long-neglected villages of the Deccan where masses of men, women, and children were without any medical or nursing care. Dr. Deena Sonna, leaving behind the allurements of the city, became physician-in-charge, and Miss Eva Logue was the nursing partner of this remarkable team.

These two pioneers did not come to the village unannounced. Before they ever undertook this venture, Dr. Sonna had visited the area and called a meeting of representatives of every group. She explained the type of service she and her nurse friend had to offer, and she asked the people to say frankly whether or not they wanted this kind of help. When they said "Yes," she laid down a basis of work that in later years became the law for every patient. Later on, when some villagers asked for special favors, the doctor had only to refer to this basis in which she had, in those early days, made it clear that everyone would be treated alike, that all who could must pay for medicines, and that only the health instruction would be given free.

The bullock cart drew up before an old mud-and-stone house that the richest man in the village had rented to the health workers. For years the building had been deserted because the villagers declared it was haunted. Now, day after day, the curious people watched as these two women settled their home. Months before, they had arranged with a Christian evangelist in Yellari to have the house made ready for use, by putting in windows, covering the earth floor with stones, white-washing the mud walls, building a chimney, and repairing the roof. This house, made liveable and attractive, became a model to all the villagers of what they could do with their own homes, at very low cost.

One of Dr. Deena Sonna's first concerns was for pregnant mothers and babies. It was a struggle against strange superstitions. Now, after fourteen years of her health service, most of the old customs relating to childbirth have disappeared from this area. The doctor delivers all babies in the homes except in case of extreme emergency. As she goes about giving the mother pre-natal care, the whole family becomes her class of instruction so that now the homes are cleaned up for the welcome arrival of the baby. Infants who used to be branded with a hot iron twelve to twenty-four times, on the third day after birth, are now spared this pain and predisposal to death. Mothers are taught proper diet and no longer suffer because they are afraid to eat. Sometimes the doctor has a fight to keep mother and child alive. Having used all her medical knowledge she has often been heard to say, "I've done everything I know. It's all up to you, Lord," and miracles happen.

Communicable diseases such as smallpox, cholera, and plague have been wiped out completely by the use of preventive inoculations. One of the biggest fights Dr. Sonna had to wage was against the guinea worm. When she and Miss Logue began work in Yellari every home had at least one person who was infected with this pest. Once a nursing infant sucked the head of a guinea worm from his mother's breast. With improved wells and the straining of drinking water, this devastating worm has been entirely eradicated, but not without opposition. Many a day a quack doctor sat throughout a morning on the dispensary veranda, urging upon the doctor's patients his own cure for guinea worm, by using roots, and cautioning them that the doctor was unable to cure their infection. When a patient would go into the treatment room the quack would follow and watch the removal of the worm. One day, after all the patients had left, the quack slyly lifted his *dhoti* to show the doctor a guinea worm in his own leg. He asked her to remove it, which she gladly did, but at the same time she gave him a lecture on his own deceitfulness.

From the beginning this Christian physician made herself one with the villagers. Many call her "Mother." They revere this woman who has done so much to change their condition of living, by teaching them about the disposal of manure, how to eliminate pests, and the necessity for immunization, sanitary wells, and septic tanks. The doctor understands their problems and their needs. She is never too busy to listen to complaints and to give advice on personal matters. The villagers hold her in awe because of her reputation as a killer of poisonous snakes. They love her because she loves both their children and their dogs. They boast about her cooking and her gardening. They pattern their simple homes after her home, and they feed their children according to her rules.

After the mud house had been used for six years as the improvised Health Center, a Brahmin gentleman came to call one day. He offered these Christian workers a plot of ground adjacent to their center so they might build a proper residence and have room to expand their work. On this ground there now stands a residence for them and their assistants, living quarters for two workers' families, a deep well with plenty of pure water, with shade and fruit trees and many flowers all around. Today the place is, in the words of Bishop Mondol, "like a beautiful lotus flower growing up from a once filthy mire." With the exception of Sundays, this center is a daily scene of action with people from near and far arriving in all sorts of conveyances, while some walk many miles to seek the doctor's help. In any one year as many as two hundred villages are represented in the patients' list. All who come, while waiting their turn with the doctor, listen to Bible stories told by the pastor, who also teaches them Christian hymns. Then one of the staff gives them a health demonstration talk while another assistant teaches them how to keep their children clean.

For months before Dr. Deena Sonna was escorted back to her village home, the people had been asking, "When will our doctor return? She has been away a long time. The village needs her." For Dr. Sonna had gone to America as a Crusade Scholar of The Methodist Church in order to learn better ways to help her Indian friends. Her aim was not to obtain another degree but to take practical courses that would give her a better grasp of public health problems and methods. Wishing to gain further knowledge in the field of obstetrics, she served first at the Margaret Hague Maternity Hospital in Jersey City. Wanting practical experience in both urban and rural work, she spent three months in the Burlington County Hospital in Mount Holly, New Jersey.

But the doctor, who cared nothing for a degree, ended up by going to the Harvard University School of Public Health, studying public health, epidemiology, sanitary engineering, and vital statistics. And in her spare time she learned to drive an auto so she could handle the new jeep given to the dispensary in Yellari. In all her practice and theory this Indian woman took high honors. With an M.A. in Public Health from Harvard, Dr. Deena Sonna returned to India, stopping in England long enough to see how socialized medicine was working.

So Dr. Sonna came back to her beloved villagers. She will never forget that welcome as the throng of admirers met her on the dusty roadside and garlanded her as if she were a queen.

To these simple people among whom the doctor has chosen to set her life, she is not a Harvard University Master of Public Health. She is their friend, who brought cleanliness and health and pure water and better homes to their dirty, dusty, pest-ridden villages, and set the love of God in their midst. In fourteen years of loving service, Dr. Deena Sonna, Christian physician dedicated to the healing of the Indian villagers, has won a place in the hearts of her people which few doctors enjoy in a lifetime of practicing medicine.

"By her life alone, the better way is shown."

From *Thirteen Biographies*, by Elizabeth Meredith Lee. Published by the Woman's Division of Christian Service, The Methodist Church, n.d. Used by permission.

The church in Southern Asia is considerably strengthened by the activities of its laymen. Noteworthy among them is the educator and scholar whose service is appreciatively reported in this article by a fellow Indian, V. M. Koshy.

Anjilvel V. Matthew

In a garage adjoining a bungalow in the heart of Bangalore, the light is on as early as five o'clock in the morning, or even earlier. In the garage are shelves of books, a table littered with typed sheets and scribbled notes, a chair by its side and another for reclining purposes. This is Anjilvel Matthew's study. He prefers the garage to his home adjoining it. Though close to three score years and ten, Dr. Matthew is a "student"; and purposeful, creative writing continues to be his passion. The early morning hour signifies his daily devotions and Bible study—a practice he has kept up all his life almost as an unalterable law of life.

It was through these quiet hours, and in unceasing and painstaking study during the day in the irrepressible spirit of his "retirement," that Matthew has just completed writing one of his most recent volumes, *Jeremiah's Life and Testimony*, a daily devotional study intended for a period of eight months and extending to nearly four hundred pages. Two companion volumes of a similar quality preceded it: *Jesus Christ, Teacher and Friend*, and *Jesus Christ, Leader and Lord*. Those who have used them have blessed him for the enlightenment and the inner glow that they have received.

The YMCA publishing house brought out another book from his versatile pen, *Psychology and Christian Education*; and a few months ago the Christian Home Department of the National Christian Council published his exposition, *How to Be Happily Married*. Having gained a profound understanding of depth psychology and having successfully reared a family of five girls and two boys, Matthew is eminently qualified to counsel others on this and allied subjects. His book, *The Child and His Upbringing*, came out earlier. Two manuscripts, *Married Life in Changing India* and *Problems in Personal Relationships* are ready for publication.

All these are but a fraction of his prolific writings. It is not to be wondered that Anjilvel Matthew has made a significant contribution to Christian education in India. His close association with the India Sunday School Union for nearly two decades has not only been of immense value to the organization, but a means of strengthening the Sunday school movement throughout this country.

Born into a highly respected ancient Syrian Christian family with sturdy evangelical traditions in "benighted" Kerala, Matthew has followed a fascinating career: teacher in a village in Kerala, two years; missionary teacher in the pan-Hindu high school in the North Kanara evangelistic field of the Mar Thoma

Church, ten years; headmaster of the Basel Mission High School, Dharwar, four years; professor and later principal of the government Teachers' Training College, Kolhapur, fifteen years; principal of the Arts College at Satara, which was an experiment in a "residential working" college, seven years; and first principal of the Teachers' Training College of the Mar Thoma Church in Central Tranvancore, one year.

This impressive list is but a skeleton outline of the herculean labors of Matthew in the field of education. He carried out these and much else in a spirit of realism, adventure, and Christ-centered devotion. By no means cut out to be an administrator, he has filled such positions of high responsibility in Christian and non-Christian schools and colleges with remarkable success, the secret of which was not red-tapism or domination, but is explained by the trite expression "friendship" in personal relationships. The period of his services to Christian institutions covered seventeen years of this working life while the remaining twenty-two years were spent among overwhelmingly non-Christian organizations. It is a tribute to his independence of spirit and deep religious convictions that everywhere Anjilvel Matthew has maintained an undiluted Christian faith.

Matthew's keen, searching mind is concerned with the whole of life—religious and secular. His is not a doctrinaire approach, for he grew with learning and weighed advances in knowledge in the light of experience. That is one great factor in his academic achievements. The University of Bombay awarded him a Master's Degree in Education after he had completed his volume on *Psychology and Principles of Education*. It received wide recognition and has been in demand for teacher's training colleges in India. As a teacher he developed a vital interest in the understanding of the human mind in its depth, known at the time as new psychology. The study of the unconscious and its mechanisms, motive forces, buried complexes and their expressions in conduct and character, the significance of dreams, neurotic behavior, maladjustment to life, and the like consumed much of his time. The sequel to this research was a voluminous book entitled *Depth Psychology and Education*. This book had the distinction of being a rare achievement among Indian scholars. It was one of the very few works, if not the only one, published anywhere that sought to work out a synthesis of the great theories of psychoanalysis of the period—those of Freud, Jung, and Adler—and succeeded in large measure.

Matthew studied Sanskrit by himself and acquired a working knowledge of it, enabling him to enjoy the treasures of Indian thought and culture from the wisdom of the Upanishads. This is an asset to which few English-educated Indian Christians can lay claim. His writings are refreshingly colored by the Sanskrit background. The range of his writings is the measure of his capacity "to see life as a whole and steadily."

Authorship undoubtedly brought him recognition that in turn urged him on to greater productivity. He was in demand for articles for periodicals; and he contributed hundreds of them to nearly fifty magazines in the course of many years. His mind conceived a variety of books. Such are his gifts that he can plan several books dealing with different subjects and develop them side by side.

Anjilvel Matthew is "friend, guide, and philosopher" equally to a variety of movements and organizations. He was closely associated with the Student Christian Movement and the National Missionary Society. A member of the Board of Studies of the Serampore College he has also been examiner for the Theological Department at almost all levels. And he has had a major responsibility for formulating the syllabus for the new degree course in religious education, which the college has initiated recently. One of his favorite enterprises, wherever he has lived, has been a discussion group for intellectuals, with all that it involved in keeping it alive and in the matter of keeping himself up-to-date on books and movements of thought. It is altogether remarkable that Matthew has found time and energy for so much fruitful activity and original writing outside his full-time professional responsibilities. An irrepressible spirit, he does not lack self-confidence and he exerts his right to think for himself. Nor will he, as a psychologist, wish to overlook the healthy, invigorating element of self and personal ambition in his crowded and eventful life. Nevertheless, the fundamental humility of a learner and seeker after truth runs through his consecrated service to the Christian cause.

Christian education and the Sunday School Movement in India are the richer for this scholar's redoubtable championship of them over these long years, and for his outstanding and devoted concern for the nurture of the young and the training of the teacher in the church in our country. We salute him as an elder statesman and thinker in this great area of Christian service.

From "Our Veteran Sunday School Leaders" in Christian Teaching, [Bangalore, India] March, 1962. Used by permission.

Countless church leaders in Southern Asia are not national figures. Yet their roles, while limited in one sense, are at the same time as meaningful as any man's can be. Some idea of the strength of the church and of the different kinds of men God is calling to the Christian ministry can be gained from these brief portraits by Ernest Y. Campbell.

Three Village Pastors

A young pastor in the Punjab has assumed almost from the beginning of his ministry a role of spiritual leader that meets the respect and approval of both his non-Christian neighbors and his parishioners. He does not emphasize going to his people, although he visits regularly. His people come to him. His residence and small church building are a spiritual center. It is known that morning and evening, whether any come or not, he will conduct worship in the church. In his approach to non-Christians, conversations are steered almost immediately into topics of vital and personal concern. His sincerity is obvious and respected. He often is asked to speak in schools and to non-Christian groups. He is involved in the trials of his people but cannot be influenced to take up questionable issues. His stand before landowners or officials is very direct and simple. The spirit of his congregation and village is confident and hopeful. The Christians of his village are a part of a church that is living and growing both in depth and in numbers. He is subject to some criticism because he does not attend church courts regularly. He is too absorbed in his own ministry to be a regular committeeman. His conversation is generally limited to the affairs of his parish and to religious issues.

Another rural pastor, with the common name of John, many miles from the first young man's village, on the western border of the state, is demonstrating an effective ministry of quite a different texture. This pastor is older. His present charge is his fourth.

John is an open, friendly man who obviously enjoys meeting people and talking to them. His interests cover all areas of rural life. There is no question as to his being a rural man or his enjoyment of rural life. He is usually accompanied by men from one or another of the fifteen villages in his parish. He lives in the village of Tibra, has six children, and keeps a buffalo and chickens. His wife is a village girl with seven years of education in mission schools. The largest group of Christians in one village in his parish comprise forty-two families. Other villages have groups of forty, twenty-six, and twenty-eight families. There are many scattered groups of from six to fourteen in his parish, which is eleven miles long and about seven miles wide.

John has recently achieved some prominence among his colleagues for initiating a system of pledges and family offering bags. His income is above that of the average rural pastor. This fact is partly explained by the large number of Christians in his congregation. This large number, however, spread out over many villages, is not always an asset. The problem of including so many, so scattered, in the life of a church has not been solved by others with similar parishes.

The secret of John's success seems to lie in his relationship to and use of his laymen. This relationship of confidence and friendship that marks John's attitude to his laymen is not only a part of his personality and temperament but the result of the response to this attitude from his people.

"I do not have anything to do with raising money," John reported. "My elders do all that. I have been emphasizing stewardship and I conduct Bible classes on the subject." When asked how he got around to fifteen villages to conduct services, he replied, "I don't. The elders and deacons conduct services when I cannot come. They know I can only get around to their village once a month—that is unless something urgent comes up."

The services in John's parish are sincere and orderly but by no means dull. He gives enthusiastic support to singing parties and evangelistic bands. Laymen lead confidently in prayer. There are often three or four Christian *sadhus*, or Indian "holy men," in his area at one time. While some pastors resent these wandering preachers and distrust their limited understanding of the faith, John seems perfectly confident of his people. His home is a public place. People are sitting in the courtyard day or night. Innumerable meals are served and the hookah is kept burning constantly and is supplied with fresh tobacco by his visitors.

His wife, a large woman with an almost boisterous good humor, joins in the steady stream of conversation in their home and acts as hostess to the men as well as the women. Much of the cooking is done by the visitors who often bring grain and occasionally vegetables or lentils.

John, with a temperament quite different from that of his saintly colleague mentioned above, seems to have found his ministry and to be the leader of a thriving and growing church by an appeal to a different facet of Punjabi character—the sociable and friendly. His people are unusually faithful in attending services and classes. They sing with outstanding vigor and have a large reportoire of psalms and hymns. Recently several nearby village groups outside his parish have asked to join his church.

Khushi Masih can be taken as typical of a group of rural padres who have assumed another role, that of undisputed community leader. Khushi Masih is a big man. He is over six feet tall and built like a wrestler. He has a deep commanding voice and his face is almost severe in its habitual expression. He has hardly been known to smile. He is often brusque in speech and aggressive in manner. He sits quietly, hardly seeming to listen, when surrounded by members of his congregation. He breaks in when he feels moved and speaks with authority and decision.

His home life is much the same as John's. The people of his rural parish, perhaps the largest in the United Church of Northern India—over one thousand souls—are in and out of his house constantly. As people come in, they greet the padre and his wife very respectfully. They nearly always bring some gift of grain or food. Khushi Masih acknowledges their greetings with dignity and asks about their families. From his questions it is evident that he knows and remembers every member of his parish.

An occasional non-Christian comes to visit or consult the padre. He is greeted with no less or no more dignity than the poorest Christian.

The obvious respect and love that his people have for him is built on much more than a gruff exterior. Khushi Masih is the acknowledged champion of his people. He is a lion in their defense and will also be blunt with the weakness of his own people. He will list their weaknesses to a visitor in the presence of his congregation, but he does not encourage any one else to criticize them. They are his people.

He has a corps of young men about him. He is looking for work for some of them—others are his assistants. He sends them with messages to different villages and calls in the elders rather than going to them. His services are partly led by these assistants. He will occasionally lead in singing and will preach with great force and conviction.

Groups come with problems from distant villages. He accompanies them to court. There seems no day goes past without the hearing, arbitration, or decision regarding some difficulty.

Khushi Masih is usually accompanied by a poet of rare gifts. Also a villager, he sums up the aspirations and concerns of his people in poems of purest metaphor. His songs have been printed and widely distributed. He softens the demanding righteousness and rigidity of his leader and friend. But there is a deep friendship and interdependence between these two men.

The people of this parish are probably poorer than the average. There are certainly fewer who have any schooling. Their life is spent in the bush country, tending isolated and poor fields and wide ranging cattle. Many physical and political inducements are presented to these poor Christians to join the scheduled castes. They are surrounded by low-caste neighbors who receive political preferment and economic advantages. Yet no Christians of this parish have given their names or recorded their faith as anything but Christian. They display a very strong devotion to their church and leader even though they are not very articulate except in their singing. As a community they are recognized to be peace loving and hard working—in a district noted for illicit distilling, cattle theft, and acts of violence.

From *The Church in the Punjab*, by Ernest Y. Campbell. (IMC Study Series on The Churches in India.) Published by The National Christian Council of India, Nagpur, 1962. Used by permission.

This short biography of P. D. Devanandan is the work of M. M. Thomas, his associate at the Christian Institute for the Study of Religion and Society, in Bangalore, India. It portrays a man of vitality and intensity whose contribution to the church was unique in nature, world-wide in value, and historic in significance.

P. D. Devanandan

Paul David Devanandan was born on July 8, 1901 in Madras, India. His parents were the Rev. Devadawson David, the son of a convert to Christianity from Madura, and Mercy David from Tanjore. Thambi, as he was called, was the third child in a devout and scholarly family. His mother is remembered even today for her love for books. She read whenever she could, and most frequently in the Bible, which she understood in Tamil, Urdu, and Telugu as well as English. Her reading gave her a steady source of inspiration to draw on in her frequent talks to the Mother's Union of the parish where Thambi's father was priest-in-charge.

Every morning and evening, parents and children had periods

of family prayer with music, with Mrs. David playing the organ and her husband the violin. The children had to memorize one verse of a hymn or a portion of the Bible and recite it daily. On Sundays the services were particularly elaborate.

These times of family worship continued for more than twenty years and their influence on the children was life-long. In 1946, visiting in the United States as an outstanding figure of the church in India, Devanandan made this note in a diary that he kept briefly: "My mind goes back to an evening in January in 1910. It is in a small room in the little house we lived in for a while in Salem. Father is away in the Punjab with the N.M.S. [National Missionary Society]. I am down with smallpox. Poor Mother is quite distracted. There is little help for her except what Mr. T. D. Moses next door can give, and Vedamuthu, our servant boy. The Pauls come now and then—they live way out in Thottam. It is time for evening prayers. Mother makes me read from St. Mark VIII, 14-29. She probably thinks of all the many illnesses, some quite serious, she had to tend me through. 'Only son' . . . 'the spirit teareth' . . . 'and often times.' There are tears in her voice when she prays: 'Lord, I believe, help thou mine unbelief.' O those prayers of my mother!"

As a child, Devanandan was tutored privately by his father until he was admitted to Thiruvallur High School, where his father was principal. He later studied at high schools in Madras and Trichinopoly. He went on to Nizam's College, Hyderabad, where he got his B.A. degree, and later won a Master of Arts degree from Madras University.

His interest in teaching as a profession had grown during the years of his own education. He taught for a time at Jaffna College, although he was still interested in further academic training. His opportunity came very shortly. In 1924 he became secretary to K. T. Paul, the famous nationalist Indian Christian leader. By mid-September of that year he was on his way to the United States with Paul. He did not return when this assignment ended, but enrolled at the Pacific School of Religion in California. After receiving his B.D. degree from that institution, he crossed the continent to study at Yale University. A Doctor of Philosophy degree in religion marked the termination of his work at Yale. His doctoral thesis on *The Concept of Māyā: An Essay . . . [on] the Hindu Theory of the World . . .* was later published in London and India.

Returning to India, he joined the staff of the United Theological College in Bangalore in 1932. It was the beginning of a seventeen-year period of notable service. He taught the history of religion and Christian ethics. His excellence as a teacher and his profound understanding of Hinduism in its traditional and renascent phases made a lasting impact on the young men who listened to him. One of these students, S. J. Samartha, now occupies Devanandan's chair at the college. He paid tribute to his former professor in these words:

"The teacher must be able to present matters clearly, concisely. Confusion in the mind of the teacher multiplies the confusion of the students. He must communicate great ideas to students effectively. And also, in the personal companionship between the teacher and the student, the teacher must so stimulate the intellectual interest of his students that they are enabled quickly to move on from the narrow confines of lecture notes to those larger and more exciting areas of original thought where the mind is without fear and the head is held high. I am sure his students will bear testimony to the fact that Devanandan possessed these qualities in abundant measure."

Devanandan loved his students and enjoyed being surrounded by them. He felt himself younger in their company. He never tolerated laziness and shoddy work, and was exacting in his academic demands. He was glad to spend time with students both in his own home and in coffee shops and restaurants. In time, a growing deafness began to trouble him and it is possible that he sought to offset feelings of depression with jests and laughter. He enjoyed playing practical jokes, and although his students and associates sometimes found them hard to bear, no friendships were broken, for he was with them as comrade and pastor.

In the same year that he began teaching at the theological college, Devanandan married Hannah Amaravathy Paul, the eldest daughter of the man with whom he had gone to the United States. The wedding took place in Salem, where he had lived as a boy, but neither of his parents was alive to participate in it. His mother had died when he was in his first year of college and news of his father's death had arrived when he was in America.

Two daughters, Nalini and Lakshmi, and a son, Marcus, were born to the Devanandans. Mrs. Devanandan died when the children were still small. In 1939, Devanandan married Checkamma Eipe, who had been teaching on the staff of the Christopher Training College. A son was born to them but lived only a few weeks.

Devanandan's deep concentration on his work and, as his career developed, his many professional responsibilities, left him little time for family life. Nevertheless, as the children grew up, a comradeship developed between them and him. They called him "Apps." He was happy to provide them with the best education they desired and deserved. It was gratifying to him when two of them chose teaching as a vocation.

Toward the latter part of his period at the United Theological College, increasing recognition was given Devanandan as a scholar and as a teacher of Hinduism and the Christian interpretation of it. He was selected to deliver important lectures at the University of Cambridge and at Selly Oak, Birmingham, in England,

and at Union Theological Seminary in New York City. He was awarded honorary Doctor of Divinity degrees by the Pacific School of Religion and Yale University. At both places, as the story goes, he missed the regular convocation and had to receive his honors in convocations specially arranged.

The present century has been a time of rising nationalism in India, and this scholar and teacher felt its stirrings in his own heart and mind. It is significant that even while in America he had changed his name from Paul D. David to Paul D. Devanandan. In the Christian enterprise in India, including his college, he was caught up in the institutional structures and behavior patterns of a colonial era. Naturally he became a rebel, although he remained committed to the church and to his work in the training of its ministry. In 1949, however, when he found the structures so rigid as to make it impossible to meet the growing financial needs of his family, he decided to leave the college. He departed without rancor or personal ill-will toward his missionary colleagues, and in later years he was frequently homesick for his teacher's chair.

For two years he served as the general secretary of the YMCA in New Delhi, and then became the director of the Department of Literature and Publication of the YMCA's of India. In 1952 he also assumed the chairmanship of the Committee for Literature on Social Concerns. Four years later he accepted the invitation of the National Christian Council of India to organize the Christian Research and Training Institute on Hinduism. In 1957 this institute was combined with the Committee for Literature on Social Concerns and the Christian Institute for the Study of Society to form a single organization. The new organization was named the Christian Institute for the Study of Religion and Society. Devanandan was appointed the director and I was named his associate.

Devanandan gave himself without reserve to an exacting program for the Institute. He was responsible for publications, consultations, seminars, and training institutes. The purpose of the program was close to his heart: to help the Indian church understand the world of religious, cultural, and social life in India, and to enter into dialogue with that world to witness to Jesus Christ as its final clue and fulfillment.

On Jesus Christ as fulfillment, he said at New Delhi in 1961: "Because the final end is totally assured, the end is in reality a present fact. In salvation-history, to the discerning eye of faith, it is the eternal future that is fulfilled in the contemporary present, not the past perfected in the future. It is in this sense our Lord declared that He had come not to destroy but to fulfill."

Devanandan's perennial theme was Jesus Christ in the "contemporary present" world of religion and society. For this reason he arranged dialogues between Christians, Hindus, and secularists on the concepts of ultimate truth, man, and society. He attended meetings of the Inter-religious Fellowship of the Friends of Truth and other groups to explain the exclusive claims of Christians as a claim for the all-inclusiveness of Christ and the Christian understanding of religious freedom. He constantly appeared before Christian groups to explain that Christ is present and active in the renascent Hindu faith and culture. This kind of presence, he said, demands that the church be spiritually discerning, that it co-operate with non-Christians in common efforts for building the nation and a national culture, and that it witness constantly to the person and work of Christ within that context. He expressed these views in two books that he wrote in this period, *Gospel and Renascent Hinduism* and *Christian Concern in Hinduism*, for which Dr. Sarvepalli Radhakrishnan, now the president of India, wrote the foreword.

He received ordination as deacon and presbyter in the Church of South India in 1954, and he took his responsibilities as minister of the Word and the sacraments very seriously. He loved to preach; there is no non-Roman congregation in Bangalore that has not heard him at one time or another. Of all the writings he has left, the only ones which are in complete form ready for publication are his many sermons.

In recent years Devanandan was keen to develop new patterns of ministry among managers, technicians, and laborers of an industrially growing society. He was at home with a group of Western and Indian executives and technicians who met in Bangalore; and one of his fruitful attempts in the recent past was to work with the Rev. Harry Daniel and other pastors to form an Industrial Workers' Fellowship in that city. He helped many young people in the universities and in lay professions to discover their own Christian vocations.

His influence outside India was considerable. He served as a consultant at many ecumenical gatherings and meetings of the World Council of Churches and the East Asia Christian Conference, especially in their study conferences. It was very fitting that he was invited to make the keynote address on Christian witness at the New Delhi Assembly of the World Council in 1961.

One or two mild heart attacks slowed him down only temporarily in the course of the last two or three years. In 1961 he had a more serious attack. He then knew the end was coming. One day last February, I began to get copies of all the correspondence and monthly statements of receipts and incomes of the Institute. He characteristically added a postscript to one: "The idea is to help you to pick up the various threads in case I pop off without notice!"

This premonition did not prevent him from undertaking exacting work in Bangalore and outside. His activities in the summer of 1962 began early in June in Alwaye, where he led a study conference of Kerala teachers and ministers on Christian participation in nation-building. He returned to Bangalore and then went to Kerala again to participate in a dialogue between Christian and Hindu friends on the concept of truth. For a few days in Trivandrum we worked on a memorandum on the policy and program of the Institute for the next five years. Then he spent a week in the Tamiland Theological Seminary lecturing to students on modern Hinduism.

In July he was at Gurukul Theological College, first to lecture to the students of the college on renascent Hinduism, and then to lead a conference of South Indian Christian theologians on the Christian doctrine of creation. He had also arranged a series of talks by Hindu scholars on the Hindu view of purpose, society, and history, so that the theologians might do their thinking on the doctrine of creation within the context of and in dialogue with Indian thought. Next, he participated in a one-day seminar of teachers from the different colleges in Madras on the contributions that the various religious and secular faiths might make to national integration and the development of a common Indian culture. In early August he went to Dehra Dun to attend a conference and after it a meeting of an Indian committee of the Danforth Foundation.

He was looking forward to leaving India with his wife on August 30 to go to Japan. He planned to teach for a year there at the International Christian University and at the same time to satisfy some of his interest in the religions and cultures of other Asian lands. But it was not to be. He died after a heart attack on August 10, 1962, at Dehra Dun.

It was fitting that three gatherings of very different nature were held in his memory. In Paris, the Central Committee of the World Council of Churches met to remember his services to the ecumenical movement. In Banaglore a service of thanksgiving commemorated his services to the Indian church and nation. In Madura members of the Gandhi Gram, a Hindu institution, met and spoke about Devanandan's concern for truth and his openness to adherents of other religions in dialogue. Significant as these occasions were, it will be as "a human person" that his many friends, Christian and non-Christian, pious and impious, will remember him.

Devanandan lived in a period of historical transition. He always sought to look forward to new and creative forces and ideas. While he was a student, theological liberalism had reduced his Christianity to a kind of religious philosophy. As a young teacher he revolted against it and found a basis for the renewal of his theology in Hendrik Kraemer's writings on Christianity's relationships to non-Christian religions. Finally, turning away from Kraemer, he began the search for a new approach to the problems of the Christian position regarding other religions, a search that led to the many dialogues that he sponsored between Hindus and Christians.

Devanandan lived the best part of his adulthood in the days of dominance by Western missions. He revolted against it but he always sought to go beyond it to the new ecumenism in mission-church and inter-church relations. In politics, he was a nationalist, but he wanted a genuine internationalism to bring "meaning-content" to his nationalism. And he saw, more clearly than anybody else of his age whom I knew, that the new period was one not of revolt but of reconstruction, whether in theological endeavor, church life, or nation-building. The Christian Institute for the Study of Religion and Society was an expression of this insight. Through it, Devanandan sought to guide young Christian leaders in their constructive task in new India, and to build them into a community of mind and spirit.

"The Light of our homes"

In the cities of Southern Asia the changing social pressures on family life are felt most acutely. James P. Alter and Herbert Jai Singh, using information from interviews in several homes, have constructed this picture of a representative middle class Christian family in India.

The Wilsons of Delhi

John and Grace Wilson are both third-generation Christians and originally from Uttar Pradesh. John's grandfather, a convert from Hinduism, was for many years a Methodist rural pastor. His father taught in a Methodist middle school in a large town. Both of John's parents are dead. A younger brother and sister live in Agra. Grace's grandfather was brought up in a Baptist orphanage and trained as an evangelist. Her father served in a Baptist hospital. Grace's mother, now a widow, lives with the Wilsons. Grace has three sisters: two live with their families in Uttar Pradesh while the youngest is a nurse in New Delhi.

John and Grace were married in 1945. They had met previously and liked each other, but the marriage arrangement was made by their parents. Prior to the wedding John had completed a two-year commercial course and secured employment as a mission accountant. Grace had just finished her training as a nurse and joined the staff of a government hospital. In 1948 they moved to Delhi where John, through the influence of friends, had obtained a higher-salaried post in a bank. Grace was able to transfer to the staff of a large Delhi hospital. John now earns Rs. 165 per month and Grace Rs. 180. Both are confirmed in their posts and receive small annual increments. Each is entitled to two weeks annual leave with pay. John has a small life insurance policy and both he and Grace contribute to pension schemes. There is no medical insurance available, but the fact that Grace is a nurse entitles her and the children to some concessions in hospital fees.

The Wilsons have three children—a girl fourteen years of age and two boys, eleven and nine. At baptism the children were given distinctively Indian names—Nirmala, Vinay, and Prakash. Nirmala attends a Christian school for girls while her brothers go to a government school near their home.

Since 1952 the Wilson family has occupied a small ground-floor flat in Devnagar, not far from the Karol Bagh Christian Colony. For this they pay Rs. 75 per month plus electricity and water charges. The landlord, a Punjabi Hindu, is now demanding Rs. 90 and threatens to evict them unless they meet his terms.

There is only one entrance to the flat—a door opening from the street into a small courtyard. To the left, as one enters, are two rooms with a narrow veranda. Beyond them, at the far side of the courtyard, are a tiny kitchen, a storeroom containing coal, wood, and other household supplies, a bathing cubicle and a bathroom with a squat-type flush toilet. (In May and June the rooms are stiflingly hot, while during the monsoons the courtyard is rain-swept and muddy.) John, Grace, and the two boys sleep in one room while Nirmala shares the other with her grandmother. Furniture is scarce—string beds, two small tables, a few straight-backed chairs and a wooden clothes closet. Extra bedding and clothing are stored in metal boxes under the beds. Each room is lighted by a single electric bulb hung from the center of the ceiling. The cement floors are bare. On the whitewashed walls hang two faded family photographs, an illustrated calendar, a peacock fan, a Sunday school print, and a "Sacred Heart" picture of Christ. Nirmala and the boys have recently added photographs clipped from film magazines. The only books besides those the children bring from school are an Urdu Bible, some old devotional books in Urdu and English, and a few tattered paperback Hindi novels. The family does not subscribe to a daily newspaper (John glances at one at the bank) but Grace occasionally buys an illustrated magazine.

In their home and at work the Wilsons speak Hindustani—basically Urdu with an admixture of Hindi and some English terms and expressions. The children are receiving their education in Hindi and cannot read Urdu. John and Grace speak and read English and are keen that their children also acquire a fluency in it.

On weekdays Grace and her mother rise by five o'clock to prepare a light breakfast of tea and *chapathis* (unleavened wheat bread) and to start cooking rice and vegetables for the morning meal. John leaves at 8:30 to join the rush of cyclists headed for work, while Grace goes soon afterward by bus. Both carry cold lunches. The grandmother feeds the children at 9:00 and sees them off to school—Nirmala in a bus and the boys on foot. The children return before their parents. Grace reaches home by 5:30 and John usually at 6:00, often having stopped in the bazar to purchase vegetables and fruit for the next day. The evening meal of meat curry, *chapathis,* and *dal* (pulse) is eaten at 8:00 and the family is asleep by 10:00.

The Wilsons live in an entirely residential area. Several city blocks are crowded with buildings similar to the one they occupy. Most of the residents are Hindus and Sikhs who migrated to Delhi from the West Punjab. Vinay and Prakash play with other boys on the paved street in front of their house. John and Grace frequently visit the only other Christian families in the neighborhood—one Anglican and the other Roman Catholic. They are on good terms with some Hindu and Sikh families but only rarely invite them into their home.

The Wilsons are faithful attendants at the Methodist church located nearly three miles from their home. John takes one of the boys on his bicycle, while Grace and the other children go by bus. Because of the time and difficulty involved in reaching the church they do not attempt to send the children to Sunday school. John's and Grace's interest in religion has grown in recent years. They find that corporate worship satisfies a deep inner need. They are proud of their religious heritage and want their children to grow up as Christians. This quickened interest also finds expression in the home. They usually say grace at meals and once or twice a week they hold family prayers after supper when Grace's mother leads in singing Hindi *bhajans* (devotional songs) and John or Grace reads from the Bible and leads in prayer. The Wilsons find that regular church attendance strengthens their ties with the Christian community and gives them a certain respect and prestige. They enjoy the opportunity of talking with friends after the service and John is very pleased at having been recently elected a member of the official board. Looking to the future, they hope that active church membership will prove an advantage in obtaining Methodist scholarships for Nirmala and the boys when they are ready to enter college. Representatives of the Methodist church occasionally come to the Wilsons' home. One of these is the church bearer who brings the subscription book to collect John's monthly pledge of Rs. 5. The pastor comes every six weeks or two months. His visit is a special occasion; tea is served and he is asked to read from the family Bible and to lead in prayer. Other visitors who come more rarely are the Methodist district superintendent and a lady missionary, one of Nirmala's teachers.

John and Grace consider themselves fortunate in many ways. Both are employed and are receiving comparatively good salaries. So far there has been no serious illness in the family. They are respected members of the Christian community and have several close friends. Nevertheless, they are troubled and anxious about several things. Vinay, a good athlete, is a very indifferent student. He has already been kept back one year in school and shows no sign of improvement. John and Grace feel that this is due to the influence of his friends, a group of undisciplined and rowdy boys. Nirmala, like many other girls her age, is a good student and well-behaved. But John and Grace are beginning to wonder whether she will find a suitable match among the Christian boys, several of whom are lazy and irresponsible. Grace's sister is a source of considerable anxiety to the family. They have heard that she spends much of her time with an older Hindu man who prefers her company to that of his wife. Grace and her mother have tried to counsel her, but she angrily threatens to break off all relations with them. The Wilsons also have financial worries. So far their income has been sufficient to meet daily expenses, but prices are rising much more rapidly than their small annual increments. They have no savings aside from the pension funds, and any emergency—such as a serious illness—would force them into debt. They are seriously concerned as to how they will meet Nirmala's college expenses two years hence. In addition to having these immediate family concerns, John and Grace feel somewhat insecure in a non-Christian neighborhood. They remember the disturbances of 1947-48 and the threats made against Christians by militant Hindus, and they are apprehensive lest their landlord appeal to communal bias in his efforts to evict them. They have talked several times of moving to another locality, but they cannot afford the rents at the Christian Colony and are not entitled to government housing.

From *The Church in Delhi*, by James P. Alter and Herbert Jai Singh. (IMC Study Series on The Churches in India.) Published by the National Christian Council of India, Nagpur, 1962. Used by permission.

The Texture of Life

Footprints of industrial workers transform a patch of earth into a momentary image of life in Southern Asia.

Simmons—Ford Foundat

The crowded, colorful vitality of city life in India is
exemplified by the traffic in an older section of Delhi.

omer Paige—Ford Foundation

This young Sikh is a partner in a
firm that manufactures bicycles.

Indians operate an American-built thresher at a mechanized farm where new agricultural techniques are tested.

Simmons—Ford Fou

The billboards of a movie house dominate a Delhi corner.

Indians play pachisi avidly; our parcheesi is similar.

nited Nations

A youngster walks by some of Nepal's countless shrines.

A hardware merchant jokes with customers in Calcutta.

The doctor, right, and the two nurses are members of the staff in a hospital at Katmandu, hub of Nepal's national life.

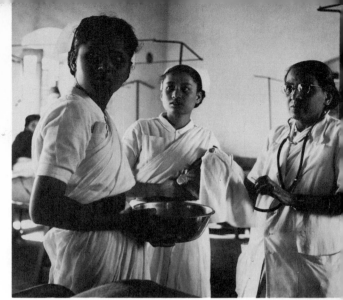

United Natio

A goal is blocked in a championship soccer game in India.

of India

Buddhists have visited this shrine in Nepal for centuries.

A holy man meditates before a Hindu temple in South India.

Blaise Levai

A Jacobite Syrian priest worships in an ancient church.

A U.N. geologist in Nepal gives an injection to an injured porter. A dead chicken hangs nearby as a sacrifice by other porters to speed their friend's recovery.

A Pakistani plows, his methods as ancient as the land.

Managers of a sugar factory in Ceylon discuss business.

Hindu pilgrims plod across a suspension bridge in Nepal.

Pakistan trains workers at this railway center in Lahore.

Indian children pause from play to gaze across rooftops in the older section of Delhi, capital of their country.

Jawaharlal Nehru is prime minister of India.

Simmons—Ford Foundation

All-India Radio reaches millions with its music programs.

Seaports such as Calcutta are vital to India's economy.

Village chiefs in India vote on a rural development plan.

A town council meets under pictures of Nehru and Gandhi.

India and Canada built this atomic reactor near Bombay.

Indian businessmen participate in a training seminar.

Spinning is a common craft among village women in India.

Brahman scholars, working at a library in Mysore, study
Sanskrit manuscripts made of palm leaves and wood.

A young businessman and his elderly accountant, working side by side, represent contrasting types in India.

Women clear land for new units of a steel mill in India.

Hand movements are important in this Ceylonese dance.

The many-windowed "Palace of the Winds" stands in Jaipur.

This Indian artist, one of the few masters of the art of brass sculpture, is ending a year of work on one statue.

Sir Rabindranath Tagore was an Indian writer whose work was widely acclaimed. It won him a Nobel prize.

A group of Pakistani schoolboys discuss United Nations activities. Asian lands give high priority to education.

United Nations

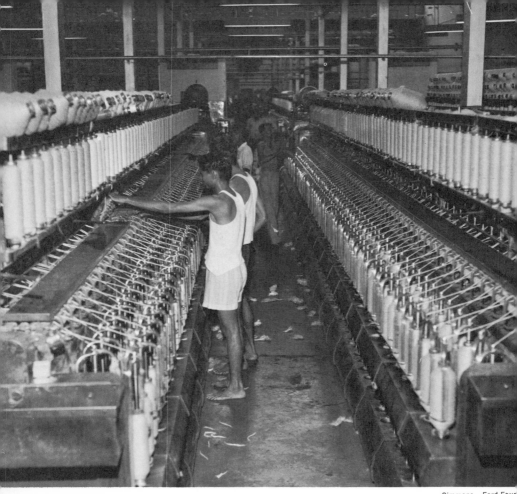

Simmons—Ford Four

The industrial development illustrated by a cotton mill
in India is changing patterns of life in Southern Asia.

Rice is transplanted in Ceylon. Population increase may exceed the island's ability to grow food for its people.

A pastoral silhouette expresses the deep relationship between Asia's farming people and the natural world.

Christians in India take particular pride in their Christian Home Movement. This activity of the church in response to the need for guidance in home and family life is described by Winifred Bryce in a discussion of part of the work of the National Christian Council.

The Christian Home Movement

A great movement within the Christian church that the National Christian Council was called upon to co-ordinate and guide was the Christian Home Movement. A few persons knew that such a movement had begun in China, but it was felt that if a similar movement were to be awakened in India it must be truly Indian, springing from the homes of the people and from practical considerations. And so it proved. It seemed to be a case of spontaneous combustion all over the country, until a central clearing house and directive body was demanded. In one province it gradually developed through a concern for social hygiene, until someone said, "Let us get at the roots of this problem, in the home." In another place the church was sensitive about the number of marriages that were taking place between educated Christian girls and non-Christian men. Again, concern was expressed by educators who felt that they had much to learn about preparing their boys and girls for future home life. Or pastors longed for help in dealing with family situations about which they were called for counsel. And always in the background was the consciousness of watching eyes that waited to appraise and judge the validity of the Christian way of life by the quality of the home life of those who were called Christians.

In response, therefore, to many requests the National Christian Council set up a Christian Home Committee, representative of men and women from different areas and various interests. A later survey made by the National Christian Council states that "the Christian Home Movement has taken root and flourished."

Three main lines of work have been carried on in this movement.

The first was in the field of literature. Bibliographies were prepared of books and pamphlets available in the major languages, as well as those written in English but with the Indian point of view. Pictures for the home have also been discovered and listed. It was found that there were seventeen Christian magazines widely read by women, and syndicated material was supplied to them. A number of bulletins had been prepared on various topics and were quickly sold out. It is known that some of the literature has made a deep appeal to non-Christians who also have a great desire for better and happier homes.

The second emphasis was in the field of education. Here again only a beginning has been made, and the field is a wide one. Theological seminaries, nurses' training schools, and teachers' training schools have been encouraged to help the students in their personal lives and also enable them to help others in the fields of opportunity they will enter. Encouragement has been given to those who are experimenting with home craft in various types of institutions. It is strongly held that this subject is for boys as well as for girls. At the request of the Christian Board of Higher Education for one of the areas, a course on family life was developed for teaching in colleges. A men's college (Lucknow Christian College) was the first place for the course to be taught experimentally and the response far exceeded all expectations. It has been given with considerable success in a number of institutions of college grade for men and women. A somewhat similar course was launched at the Ewing Christian College in Allahabad.

Third and most important of all, the Christian Home Movement has in many places been integrated with the work of the local church. In refresher courses for pastors, advice on counseling has been given, and the preparation of Christian young people for marriage has been discussed. But the outstanding way of relating the Christian Home Movement to the membership of the church in town or village is the dramatic and appealing Festival of the Christian Home, which is being more and more widely observed. There has been nothing mechanical about it, but it has become part of the life of the church. The cleaning and decorating of the house, and perhaps a gift to the house of a plant or a picture, some family fun, a special family Sunday in church, and above all the dedication of the home in a festival of lamps, in true Indian style, are features of the observance. In Dornakal Diocese, where the Festival originated, it is enthusiastically observed in many villages in this way and often includes a procession of both men and women around the village to pray for God's blessing on each home. In one church a lamp for each household in the congregation was lighted at the evening service. The whole chapel was flooded with a blaze of light and the congregation cried aloud the three-fold response:

Christ is the Light of the World;
Christ is the Light of our Homes;
Christ is the Light of our Life.

Then the head of each house came forward to the sanctuary steps and received his light from the cross to take home.

One Christmastime the Christians of many villages were gathered together, to think and pray about their homes. The evening service was unforgettable. Like the lamps, each little home represented there seemed very ordinary and rather inadequate for the witness it was called upon to give to the glory of God in everyday life. The wind of persecution or the cares of the world seemed likely to extinguish the flickering flame. But the little lights seemed to be strengthened by being gathered together, and placed as they were what a lovely radiance they gave! And so, perhaps more than anything else—more than by the councils and organizations that have been set up—by the Christian homes to which all these are but ministers, will be manifest the glory of God. In all their human frailty has been manifested the love of God, as it was shown supremely in the Incarnation.

Adapted from *India at the Threshold,* by L. Winifred Bryce. Published by Friendship Press, New York, 1946.

The changes that are affecting society in Southern Asia are being felt even in the strong relationships of family life. The dangers and opportunities for Christians are outlined by James L. H. Amarasekara of Ceylon.

Ceylon: The Family and the Church

A new day has dawned for the church in Asia. It brings tremendous opportunities with the changing patterns in Asian life. In these changing patterns there are two important tasks bearing on the family for the church in Ceylon. The first is to recover the significance of the Christian family in the church's life and witness. The second is to make the conversion of family groups the church's primary aim in evangelism.

The concept of individual salvation naturally led the early Western missions in Asia to seek individual conversions. Converts were drawn apart from their families; coming under Western influences, they adopted an increasingly Western way of life. Christian communities grew and developed apart from the larger community of non-Christians surrounding them. In some countries, in advantageous circumstances, Christians held themselves in "splendid isolation" from their fellow nationals, and were divorced from the culture and aspirations of their nation.

In recent years the position has been reversed. With the resurgence of nationalism and of non-Christian religions in these newly independent countries, the Christian communities have been looked upon and made to feel as alien minorities in their own lands. The challenge has shaken the churches to a sense of reality; the pressing need is to become rooted in the soil of each country. The churches of these countries are becoming more aware of a common life. They are beginning to discover themselves as part of an Asian church with its own mission.

In no respect is this more true than the place of the family in the church's policy of evangelism. That policy is not to dislodge individuals and disrupt families, but rather to convert whole families and family groups within the national structure.

Hitherto the fellowship of the church has been thought of as a congregation of individuals, rather than of families. Churches have judged themselves by their institutional or numerical strength rather than by the quality of life and witness of their families, under God. Today the churches in these lands are aware that, in some countries at least, Christian homes may be all that will be left to them. They are being roused to a new awareness of the significance of the Christian family to the life and witness of the church as the family of families.

The Christian family can be the most potent agency for evangelism in its non-Christian neighborhood, with all its opportunities for personal interaction. There is a double task here. One part is for the church to work out the contribution it has to make to the Christian family. The other is to educate the Christian family on the contribution it must make to the church.

The temptation to look inward and close in upon itself is ever present to a minority community. But the Christian community must ever be the salt and the leaven where it is placed. It must look outward, and seek to infuse its life throughout the nation as a whole. The present is the church's hour of opportunity.

Changes that have come over family and home in Western countries during the past 150 years are steadily sweeping over Asia as well. Asian family life is fast changing. This is affected by the emancipation of women, the increase of industrialization, with attendant improvement of transportation and communication, and the consequent extension of cities and the urbanization of villages.

Under these new pressures, the old patriarchal family pattern is slowly but steadily breaking up. Young working people mix and move about more freely. They are removed from parental authority and from family convention. They are increasingly free to marry partners of their own choice and to set up homes of their own.

There are trials in this new way of living. Temptations come through unemployment, housing shortages, unhealthy commercialized influences. These trials and temptations, of which their parents were ignorant, call for a tougher moral fiber to face the attendant responsibilities. Career women have less time for their homes and the duties of motherhood. Children suffer from the deprivation of their mothers; their physical, mental, and spiritual foundations are laid while in the care of substitute parents, employed more under pressure of necessity than for suitability. There are various results of living under these conditions: increasing divorce rates, broken homes, rising delinquency.

The secular state is concerned about these problems, too. In many countries of Asia, commissions have been appointed to study the situation and to suggest remedial measures. This could be a fruitful field for the church, not only among Christians, but among non-Christians as well. The church can give a lead in providing marriage guidance and family life education at the national level; such services will be readily welcomed in the present context, and with the ever-increasing population.

The task is immense. It calls for informed and discerning leadership. Happily the churches are coming alive both to their responsibilities and to their opportunities for family life.

From "A New Quality in Family Life," by the Ven. James L. H. Amarasekara, in *World Christian Education,* Fourth Quarter, 1959. Used by permission.

"To have a church"

A uniquely Southern Asian expression of church life is the Christian ashram or retreat. While it is not a new development, it is receiving fresh attention today as a means of deepening the spiritual life of the Christian community and of sharing the gospel with those who are seeking God. This account of the place of the ashram in Indian life and its Christian adaptation was written by Eddy Asirvatham.

The Ashram

An ancient religious institution of India, known as the ashram, is certain to play an important part in making Christianity indigenous to this land. It is not an institution in the ordinary sense of the term. It is an organism, rather than an organization, and it is admirably suited to the religious conditions of India. The ashram is loosely organized around a guru, or spiritual teacher, who has reached the third stage of life according to the Hindu idea of a good life, which is the stage of the forest-dweller.

In setting up an ashram, the guru frees himself from earthly cares and devotes himself to prayer, meditation, study, instruction, and spiritual discipline. Disciples gather around him and live together a more or less communal life. While the guru is the center of the ashram, he does not exercise the authority of an abbot or of the head of a monastery. He is an older brother instructing the younger ones in spiritual exercises and discipline.

In contrast to a monastery, the ashram is non-authoritarian. No rigid discipline is maintained. While a few who constitute the core of the ashram may impose rigid rules upon themselves, the rest are more or less free to follow their inclinations within the general framework of the ashram. Prevailing informality makes it possible for enquirers and those buffeted by the world to come and stay as long as they choose. Ample scope is provided for unhurried prayer and reflection and for the deepening of the spiritual life. No set forms are prescribed. Each member of the ashram contributes to its maintenance through some form of manual labor. Life is very simple. *Ahimsa*, or non-injury, implying love and friendliness to all, is a cardinal principle of the ashram. With it goes *asanga*, or nonattachment to material things, to binding secular relationships, and to desire for the fruits of labor. Thirst for material goods and gratification of the senses are left behind.

The ashram is a co-operative colony in every sense of the term. Members are linked together by a common desire to discover truth. All ashrams are not of a spiritual or religious nature. There have been, and still are, ashrams for secular and scientific purposes. Some of the ancient ashrams of India developed free thinking and even agnosticism.

The ashram is nonsectarian and undenominational. It does not prescribe creedal or denominational tests. Every seeker after truth is welcome. The common goal is God-realization and realization of oneness with one's fellowmen. Special emphasis is laid on a life of silence and meditation. The ashram is free from all traces of traditionalism, ritualism, or sacerdotalism. There is no priesthood, no hierarchy, but only laymen. The ashram at its best is a spiritual powerhouse, a laboratory of spiritual experimentation. Each member is encouraged to seek God in his own way. All are knit together by ties of spiritual kinship. Such ties enable members to reach a high degree of integration. In order not to live entirely for themselves, members render service to the neighboring community.

The ashrams of ancient India were forest ashrams, which can trace their history back at least 2,500 years. It is more than likely that the great Hindu epics, the *Ramayana* and *Mahabharata*, were written in ashrams. Ashrams did not all follow the same pattern. While much attention was given to prayer and contemplation, many of the ashrams devoted themselves to practical work.

With the ascendency of Buddhism, ashrams were gradually replaced by monasteries, although they never disappeared completely. It is only in modern times, however, that ashrams have been revived on a large scale and adapted to the changing conditions and needs of the day. *Santiniketan,* abode of peace, established by Rabindranath Tagore in 1901 a few miles away from Calcutta, is an educational and cultural ashram, now being developed into a university. It seeks "to recapture some of the elements of Indian culture that are fast disappearing under conditions of modern civilization" and to fuse them with elements of value in a world culture. Gandhi's ashrams at Sabarmati and at Wardha have been ashrams of social and political action, emphasizing *ahimsa,* or non-injury, in thought, word, and deed. Plain and simple living, continence and poverty, with service to the rural masses, especially through a revival of village industries, are the governing passion. The usual vows taken are the vows of continence, of truth, of *ahimsa,* of the control of the palate, and vegetarianism, of non-stealing, and the vow of fearlessness. Aurobindo Ghose's ashram at Pondicherry is of a different type altogether. It is an ashram for religious mystics and for those seeking the meaning of reality largely from the speculative standpoint.

During the past thirty years, through the impetus given by Sadhu Sundar Singh, ashrams among Indian Christians have come into vogue. They are an indigenous expression of Christianity and are, in some ways, an answer to the non-Christian charge that Christianity in India is a foreign religion. There are ashrams for unmarried men, for unmarried women, and for both married men and women.

For long years, there has been a feeling on the part of many that the work in the church was becoming highly organized and mechanized and that there was not enough fellowship and equality among Christian workers. Also, racial and economic differences were permitted to arise, which, in the church, defeat the growth of love in its initial stage. The ashram movement began as a corrective and continues to grow.

Though essentially a place of prayer and worship, the Christian ashram is not an asylum for recluses. Refuting the idea that the ashram may become isolated from common life, Mr. A. C. Chakraverti, himself the founder of a Christian ashram, says: "In an ashram we live the full life, the whole life or nothing at all."

Some ashrams are nondenominational, while some are interdenominational. According to Mr. S. Selvaratnam, the founder of a Christian ashram in Ceylon, the ashram, though not a handmaid of the church in a narrow sense, has no existence outside the context of the church. In many ways it is the vanguard of Christianity, moving into areas of life and into places that are ordinarily closed to the church. Renunciation is the key principle, as against the "professionalism" of the church. In the words used by the Ecumenical Studies on Evangelism in India: "The Christian desire to participate in a life of renunciation touches the Hindu at a place of real understanding. The ashram offers more than a service to the community; it is service in a medium that is natural to the Hindu religious life." In the circumstances prevailing in India, the ashram may well become the spearhead of an unpaid lay ministry, suited to Indian conditions and appealing to Indian sentiments. Dr. P. D. Devanandan, quoted in the Ecumenical Studies, says, "Our system of the paid ministry leads the non-Christian to think that our zeal is largely founded on the material benefits that go with our profession of faith. We need to prove to our non-Christian friends that the work of the church and the spread of the faith literally do not pay."

Among foreign missionaries, Dr. E. Stanley Jones has done much to popularize the ashram ideal. His ashram, however, is not a year-round institution and there is no guru constantly living with his *sishyas*, disciples. It is primarily a spiritual retreat for Christian workers, with a sprinkling of non-Christians, the emphasis being on study, discussion, prayer, and meditation, physical labor, and brotherly living. Limited *ahimsa*, simplicity of life and standards, and racial equality are practiced.

The best illustration of an Indian Christian ashram is the Christu-kula Ashram, the family of Christ, at Tirupattur in South India. Like the ancient ashrams of India, it is multipurpose in character. It is not only a place of worship and spiritual search, but a medical, rural reconstruction, educational, and evangelistic center. The doctors in charge are skilled, deeply spiritual men. They work and worship side-by-side, the community centering around the *japalaya*, or house of prayer. Dr. Jesudasan, the "elder brother" as he is popularly called, who has a flair for Tamil music, has compiled a book of prayers and a book of lyrics suited to the needs of the ashram. Some members observe *sashtanga*, prostration, when they pray. Nearly all habitually wear khaddar, the coarse white homespun cloth woven by the villagers. The diet is vegetarian. The two doctors, together with a third who has recently joined the inner circle, keep in close touch with the church and with Christian youth movements, and they frequently travel among, and speak to, Christian people. The ashram is not affiliated with any denomination.

Workers remain in the ashram for one to five years or more. Some are qualified doctors. Students with an ardent desire to serve come for summer vacation and work for board and lodging. No appeal is made for funds. The only appeal is for voluntary workers. What makes ashrams of this kind unique is the quality of life lived by their members.

Although the ashram illuminates some of the weaknesses of the church, it is not meant to supplant the church. As Dr. Immanuel observes, while the church has regulative value, the ashram has creative value. The two happily supplement each other. In the nature of the ashram, its informality and its unmistakably spiritual character make a greater appeal to the religious-minded Hindu than does the well-organized church with its face so often turned toward the West.

If the ashram is not meant to replace the church, neither is it meant to replace the Christian ministry. It can well contribute to the work of theological schools in its power to deepen the spiritual lives of students, as well as to give them a passion for devoted service, especially in rural areas where the majority of people live. A danger lies in solitariness, stoicism, and asceticism. But since brotherly concern and social service are active tenets of most ashrams, it is not likely that otherworldliness will become an end in itself.

From *Christianity in the Indian Crucible*, by Eddy Asirvatham. Published by YMCA Publishing House, Calcutta, 1955. Used by permission.

The Christians of Southern Asia are concerned that other Asians see the church as something that belongs in Asia and not something imported from the West. The problem for the church is to put down its roots in the culture and yet not to adapt to the extent that the truths of the Christian faith are distorted or lost. Sydney Weragoda of Ceylon interprets the problem as it relates to the church in his country.

Ceylon: Christid in Culture

To worship God in accord with the culture and customs of our peoples would be indigenous worship. To think of, and to preach about, God in harmony with the thought forms of these peoples would be an attempt to make the doctrines of our faith at home here. Care must be taken, of course, not to lose the universality of Christianity. Nor should we follow local patterns so slavishly as to be in danger of syncretism. But adaptation is inherent in the life of the church. It can be truly said that the Incarnation is an expression of what is "indigenous." For through the Incarnation, God expressed himself in the language of humanity.

Although adaptation is spontaneous and inherent, there is

need for a deliberate encouragement of the process. Some think that indigenous worship is worship in the vernacular, the language of the people. It is more than that. Where the gifts and culture of our people are embodied in our worship, it is indigenous worship.

We have seen a farmer worship his hoe before cutting his first sod for the day. The mason does the same thing to his trowel before he starts his day's work. The bus driver takes the same attitude at his steering wheel. They do not know what they worship; theirs is an "unknown God." What they worship as unknown, Christians ought to know. But alas, even a working Christian does not recognize God in his everyday life and action.

If the worshiper's rhythm of everyday life reflects the culture he is used to and his worship of the known God manifests the sense of awe common to his people, then his worship has been fundamentally adapted to his own natural mode of life. Since worship and life are so inextricably interconnected, we naturally go to the worship of the church to see how far we have been able to make worship a part of the common life.

One of the forms of indigenous worship is expressed through architecture. An example is the chapel at the Training Colony, Peradeniya, Ceylon. In similar mode is the chapel of Trinity College in Kandy; it adapts to Christian use the traditional structures of this culture. Other architectural examples are found in the Church of Christ of the Risen Lord at the University of Ceylon, Peradeniya, the Cathedral Church of Christ the King, at Kurunegala, and Christ Church at Baddegama.

There are other features, too, in attempts to assure that worship in Ceylon's churches is indigenous:

1. Language. It goes without saying that the vernacular tongue is essential for making the worshiper at home in his worship.

2. Music. The entire liturgy of the church has been set to music native to Ceylon. For the last thirty years, lyrics to local melodies have been used here. There are special lyrics for children, and a complete church hymnal with oriental music has been prepared. Local instruments are used, too—the *esraj*, the *tambura*, local drums, and so on. These give wonderful richness to the music of liturgy and hymns.

3. Posture. It is indigenous to Ceylon to be seated on the ground for worship, instead of in pews. Greetings in the service, such as the kiss of peace, is done in the local way. There are prostrations at solemn moments of the Eucharist. These all give a richness to indigenous worship.

4. Lamps and lights. On the altar, instead of the usual candles, brass lamps in oriental design are used.

5. Native handicrafts. Needlework, carvings, art of our own people are lavishly used in the decoration of the furniture and the vestments of the church.

In endeavoring to adapt the worship of the church we have tried to connect intimately the life of the people with God. But as yet, out of a Christianity taught in forms not natural to the people, there has not emanated a truly indigenous attitude in worship.

I remember seeing once the fervor with which devotees approached the sacred precincts of a Buddhist temple near Kurunegala. The ascent to this sacred place was steep. Yet how the lame hobbled up! How the aged and hunched pilgrims ascended! How the mothers with infants in arms, and pregnant women, struggled upward! And as they approached the caves that housed the statues of the Buddha, I am sure the atmosphere gave them something more than mere devotion to a dharma or teaching. It was for them a devotion to a personal Buddha. Even to us as onlookers came a sense of awe through the scent of jasmine and camphor, wafted across from the *mal asanas* or flower altars.

That is what we seek to bring to our people when we baptize them to faith in Christ; until we achieve that intensity, we can move our people but little. Their inner being is unmoved at the soulless imitations of a worship fundamentally alien.

All is not lost, though. Gradually the spirit of worship in our own way is creeping in. The atmosphere of our own culture will soon come with a growing awareness among us Christians that we have to speak to our people in a language they can understand.

From "Indigenous Worship in Ceylon's Churches," by Sydney Weragoda, in *World Christian Education*, First Quarter, 1959. Used by permission.

The task of Christian witness in Southern Asia has impelled the churches toward a unity that is a pioneering effort not only for them but for all the churches in the world. Dr. Scopes reports on the aspect of this effort that has led to the formation and growth of The Church of South India. Similar plans for union are now before the churches of North India and the churches of Ceylon.

Division and Unity

Christians in the West are often unaware that the multiplicity of denominations associated with the Protestant missionary enterprise has resulted in an intensification of that pattern on the mission field. In Great Britain the major denominations may be comparatively few, but they are duplicated in the Commonwealth countries, and if there are few from the European continent there are many from the U.S.A. The latest edition of *The Christian Handbook of India* lists more than two hundred church and mission bodies. Those of us who have lived long in India tend to relate local geography to the Christian enterprise, just as members of a large business firm think of places in terms of their branch offices and representatives. When I think of

Tirunelvely, my immediate reaction is to recall the work of the Church Missionary Society and the Society for the Propagation of the Gospel. When Trivandrum is named I think of the London Missionary Society and the Missouri Synod Lutherans; if Bilaspur, then the Disciples; if Raipur, the Evangelical and Reformed mission; if Poona, the boards of the Church of Scotland, the American Methodists and Congregationalists. These mental reactions tend now, of course, to relate to the churches formed in such places rather than the missionary societies.

The Church of South India is by far the largest in the south, embracing people who speak four Dravidian languages—Malayalam, Tamil, Kannada, and Telugu. It continues the Christian witness begun by a number of missionary boards and agencies from Europe, North America, and Australia.

As one moves up to the central belt of India one encounters four other main languages, Oriya, Marathi, Gujarati, and Hindi. The last named is now being made the national language. Children in other areas learn it in school in addition to their mother tongue. Hindustani, Punjabi, and Urdu in the north have affinities with Hindi.

The United Church of Northern India, whose most southerly point is Nagpur, brings together groups related to Presbyterian and Disciples churches, the United Church of Christ and the United Church of Canada, and several British societies.

Nobody can read even a summary of the statistics dealing with the activities of the Christian church without being impressed by the total impact made on the life of India. All this is the outcome of the way in which the missionary movement has been developed over a period of a century and a half.

During August, 1960, we celebrated the golden jubilee of "Edinburgh, 1910," which has long stood out as a landmark in ecumenical church history. Two outstanding leaders at that memorable 1910 conference were John R. Mott and V. S. Azariah, both of whom were able to speak with the knowledge of what had been happening in India. Long before the close of the nineteenth century, Christian leaders belonging to different churches had felt impelled to draw together in fellowship for counsel and prayer. This led to a conscious need for an all-India organization to promote corporate thinking and discussion of common problems and to make possible joint action. Thus, following Edinburgh, 1910, an all-India organization quickly came into being with the establishment of the National Missionary Council, some years later reconstituted as the National Christian Council. This council now has thirteen affiliated councils in the various language areas, some with full-time secretaries. It can speak on behalf of 5 million non-Roman Christians on large questions affecting the community. In addition to co-ordinating Christian activities (evangelism, education, literature, theological education, medical work, economic life, and many others), it undertakes studies and surveys on behalf of the churches, and through its monthly magazine, *National Christian Council Review*, it seeks to stimulate thought and action in constructive ways.

It is evident that this kind of co-operation has been a major factor in movements towards organic union in the church. Other factors include the rise of nationalism, the desire of Indians to have a church of their own, the sensitiveness to the charge of disunity in proclaiming a gospel purporting to offer reconciliation, and a consciousness that as a small minority Christians must stand together. Westerners ought not to be surprised that Christians belonging to the younger churches do not feel the same intense loyalty to denominational beliefs and practices, the origin of which they know little about. There is deep gratitude and abiding affection as they think about the particular missionary society through which they came to know the gospel. But obviously the call for fellowship comes strongest from those who are physically closer and who profess the same essential faith.

The way of organic union has not proved easy. It took twenty-eight years of patient negotiation before the Church of South India came to birth. Much has been written about this church and how those who formerly belonged to Episcopal, Presbyterian, Methodist, and Congregational branches of the church have found joy and newness of life together. Some personal testimony, however, may not be out of place.

There were, I think, two main factors that changed my own attitude to the church union movement in South India from skepticism to eager support. The first was an uneasy conscience over the church situation in the areas where I served as a district minister within a few years after appointment. I was stationed at Jammalamadugu in the more southern part of Andhra, and with the help of one ordained Indian minister I was responsible for the welfare of about sixty village congregations within a radius of some fifteen miles. These second and third generation Christians came from that section of the *harijans* called the Malas, and their coming over to the Christian church was the outcome of the work of the London Missionary Society. Interspersed with these village groups (of anything from ten to sixty families) were other village groups here and there that had been established by the Society for the Propagation of the Gospel before rules of comity came into existence. These Christians also were formerly Malas. Thus before the coming of the gospel all the Mala hamlets in that district were one, economically, socially, and religiously. They are still one, economically and socially; they continue to intermarry. But in the course of two or three generations of Christianity some are now stamped with an L.M.S. pattern in worship and outlook, while the rest are unmistakable S.P.G.

This would not matter if it did not lead to a wall of division at the Lord's table. Did not Jesus Christ come "to break down the middle wall of partition"? Yet his acceptance has brought about an opposite effect among a people originally one. How is it possible to preach a gospel of reconciliation in such a situation?

The second factor was membershp over a period of years in the joint committee that negotiated the plan of union. In the first place I came really to know representatives from the other churches. I discovered a quality of fellowship that warmed my heart. Moreover, the guiding hand of God upon us was unmistakably evident. Occasions arose when our discussions on difficult issues of faith and order led to an impasse and when individually and as groups we had to say, "Here we stand; we can do no other," and it looked as if negotiations would have to be broken off. Then as we paused, desolate in spirit, some member would see a new approach to the particular problem that would renew hope and lead on to a solution. This happened time after time through the years and we could not but rejoice in the clear evidence of the Holy Spirit's guidance. We began to say to ourselves, "This movement is of God."

To be sure, in the latter stages other factors also operated to bring us together. But the high levels of fellowship and experience of the Holy Spirit's power enjoyed by the negotiators prepared the way for that newness of life that many observers have noted at C.S.I. synod meetings.

This new church has been fortunate in its leadership, both national and foreign. Unquestionably their coming together from various ecclesiastical traditions in an exciting adventure has engendered a youthful courage to face up to the challenges of today in modern India. As a secretary of the National Christian Council, I formed the impression that no church in India is more alert than the C.S.I. to its essential task.

But what of the local congregations? To what extent have they been affected by being in the new church? It must be admitted that little change so far is visible in areas where there is no intermingling of traditions at this level. The Kistna diocese, for instance, is solidly ex-Anglican, and in such areas, whatever the tradition, it is difficult to overcome rural conservatism even to the extent of introducing new liturgical forms of worship. Only in the larger local groups has the C.S.I. become really meaningful. Greater progress may be expected as more and more clergy trained in the united theological institutions take the place of those belonging to an older generation. Such institutions are now found in all four South Indian language areas and notably in the United Theological College at Bangalore.

In areas where more traditions than one are present the fruits of the union are more apparent. For example, the pre-union diocese of Dornakal, now limited in size, consists in part (50 per cent) of an area previously connected with Medak (Methodist), which has recently supplied the new Indian bishop. At Dornakal itself local parish life was enriched some years ago by the organization of Methodist class meetings and the Congregational church meeting. This came about through the initiative of the then ex-Anglican bishop in consultation with members of the staff in the local theological college, who represent all three traditions.

Much is obviously to be gained by the mingling of the C.S.I. traditions at the local level. Yet on account of the necessary continuance of Western support such mingling also constitutes a problem. The supporting missionary societies vary in policy and in the degree of support they are anxious or able to give financially to different types of work. Thus even within a diocese there occur variations in standards and scales of pay in medical, educational, as well as pastoral work, which cause difficulty. Serious attention is being given to this both in South India and in the West.

In recent years the Church of South India has started conversations for wider union with five Lutheran churches in South India. There is now agreement by an inter-church commission that there exists no fundamental differences in basic Christian doctrine. A draft statement of faith has been unanimously adopted for the consideration of the churches concerned. Steps are being taken to bring about closer fellowship and the use of a common catechism. The actual work of drafting a constitution for a new United Church is underway.

Meanwhile attention is being focused on North India, where several large denominational churches, including Episcopalians, Methodists, and Baptists, as well as the present United Church of Northern India have been in conversation and negotiation for many years and have reached a stage when a final decision is expected to be made shortly. It is gratifying that in all these movements an attempt has been made to conserve all that is of value in the various traditions, following the principle of "comprehensiveness." This ensures that the experience of the church distilled in the process of heartbreaking divisions will not be lost.

It is indeed noteworthy that in the difficult problem of uniting episcopal and non-episcopal traditions, India is giving a lead to the churches of the West.

From *Indian Opportunity*, by Wilfred Scopes, with adaptations by the author. Published by The Edinburgh House Press, 1961, London. Used by permission.

CONCLUDING OBSERVATIONS

A college girl in Katmandu remarked recently that "the changes that are taking place in Nepal are probably good, but they are coming too fast. It would have been better if they could have been spread over a period of one hundred or two hundred years instead of being squeezed into ten or twenty."

Her words apply with almost equal force to the other nations of Southern Asia. Patterns of life throughout the area are changing swiftly. People are migrating from villages to already swollen cities. They are turning from the land to work in factories. They are abandoning the ancient ties of family.

Viewed from another perspective, the transformation is being shaped by the efforts of India, Pakistan, Nepal, and Ceylon to develop a sense of national unity among their peoples. Another influence is each nation's struggle for a stronger economy. Both of these forces are invigorated by the belief of 500 million people that they have a right to expect the benefits that modern civilization can bring in security, comfort, and opportunity. The ancient religions, responding to these currents, have become revitalized.

The nations of Southern Asia are not involved in these critical engagements in isolation from one another or from the rest of the world. The dispute between India and Pakistan over Kashmir is an example of the way in which neighbors can complicate one another's lives. India has been helped by United Nations programs; some of her troops were serving with UN forces in Africa while she was trying to defend her northeast border against Communist Chinese invaders.

This complexity of peoples and problems is the area in which the church in Southern Asia is living today. And while the church feels that it may have answers to give, it knows that it has its own questions to raise.

The first inquiry that Christians make of themselves is, "Do we belong? Does the church in Southern Asia live in creative relationship to its environment?"

In the Western world, the church stands in a fairly clear, if not always redemptive, relation to culture. But in India, Pakistan, Ceylon, and Nepal, the church is still something fundamentally strange, burdened with the need to demonstrate that it is not a foreign institution.

The Christian Institute for the Study of Religion and Society is an example of how the church in India is trying to relate itself more effectively to its environment. Its program has drawn the interest of non-Christians as well as Christians. Yet church leaders recognize it as only a first step in witnessing. One of the great needs of this hour in Southern Asia is to find ways by which the Institute's discoveries will be acted out in the everyday life of the church.

A second question in the hearts of Southern Asia's Christians is, "Does the church have a unique mission and message?" They feel, as never before, the need to clarify their faith, both for themselves and for their fellow men. Loud and persistent voices challenge them with the assertion that all religions are alternative and optional ways to one goal. The life or death of the church hangs on the beliefs that Jesus lived and died under Pontius Pilate and that "God was in Christ reconciling the world to himself."

A third question often heard in the councils of the church in the four lands of our concern is a familiar one everywhere: "What does God require of us in these times?" A Christian from Ceylon spoke for his fellows throughout Southern Asia when he wrote, "In our country, we are in the midst of a revolution, a ferment of new ideas and new attitudes. What does it mean to be a Christian in such a context?"

Some response to these questions seems to be appearing. Christians in Southern Asia realize that, while the gospel of Christ is, in a sense, always foreign, the Holy Spirit teaches his people what to speak wherever they are. Many of them are convinced that the gospel will be effectively expressed in Asian culture by first of all listening to the Holy Spirit and seeking to do his will in contemporary situations.

Southern Asia's Christians increasingly are seeing themselves as a missionary community. Where once there was the tendency to withdraw from the world, there is more and more the vision of the church as the chosen people of God, called together for a mission to all men. In this view, the layman's role is seen to be as important as the ordained minister's.

The movement toward church unity is another direction of growth. The article by Dr. Scopes, "Division and Unity," tells what has been accomplished. But leaders of the church in Southern Asia believe that much remains to be done. Plans for church union in Ceylon and North India have suffered setbacks that may delay them twenty years. Although these leaders know from the experience of forming the Church of South India that church union develops slowly, they feel a sense of urgency. To them, the matter has to do with the very unity of the body of Christ, and they know that a divided witness cannot match the power of men's other faiths.

It is of special concern to Christians in North America that church union in Asia has been made difficult by denominational relationships with the rest of the world. In the past, these ties have been a source of great strength. But today a local congregation sometimes is torn between two desires: it wants to become a part of the united church in its area but it also wants to maintain its connection with the denomination that gave it birth. D. T. Niles has told of two brothers, converted from Hinduism, who became members of two different Protestant denominations while in college; when they returned to their village they were unable to take communion together.

This particular problem is only one of the many confronting the church in Southern Asia that also touch the lives of Western Christians. Our common faith binds us to one another. Our concern for the witness of Southern Asia's Christians is the feeling that members of a closely-knit family have for one another. They and we, and all other Christians, make up the body of Christ.

The sharing of gifts has not been at all one-sided between Southern Asian and North American Christians. In the matter of theology alone, Southern Asia has given bountiful gifts to the church in the West.

New avenues of missionary work are being explored in Southern Asia. Leaders of different denominations are urging their churches to join forces to make a united witness. At the same time they are encouraging the church in the West to shift from denominational patterns of work to what has been called "Joint Action for Mission." One outcome of this effort may be that North American Christians will be called upon to support missionary work directed toward building one Christian church in Southern Asia rather than separate, denominational churches.

Does this interest imply that missionaries from the West are still needed? Korula Jacob, secretary of the National Christian Council of India, expressed a widely held point of view when at the 1961 assembly of the World Council of Churches, he said:

"It is often said that the younger churches should bear the main responsibility for the evangelization of the people of their lands. While this has an element of truth in it, it is manifestly beyond these churches to discharge this duty by themselves. Many of the churches are not as alive to their responsibility as they ought to be. . . . For this and for supplementing their own limited resources in personnel, the younger churches need fellow workers from the older churches."

The church in Southern Asia and those who have stood beside it can be encouraged by the progress that has been made in recent years; but in the Christian mission, success must always be measured in terms of what remains to be done. When we remember that nearly 500 million people in Southern Asia do not know Christ, and that vast areas of man's life are unclaimed by his lordship, it becomes painfully clear that by far the greater part of the road for the Christian mission lies ahead.